trompe l'oeil

trompe l'oeil

murals and decorative wall painting

Lynette Wrigley

For Theo
and Mary

This edition first published in 2002 by
New Holland Publishers (UK) Ltd
London · Cape Town · Sydney · Auckland
www.newhollandpublishers.com

Garfield House, 86-88 Edgware Road, London W2 2EA, United Kingdom

80 McKenzie Street, Cape Town 8001, South Africa

Level 1, Unit 4, 14 Aquatic Drive, Frenchs Forest, NSW 2086, Australia

218 Lake Road, Northcote, Auckland, New Zealand

ISBN 1 85368 929 7 (pb)

2 4 6 8 10 9 7 5 3 1

Editor: Helen Varley
Designer: Peter Crump
Editorial assistant: Joanna Ryde
Editorial Direction: Yvonne McFarlane

Reproduction by Modern Age Repro House Ltd., Hong Kong
Printed and bound in Singapore by Tien Wah Press (PTE.) Ltd.

Front cover, left: The Cloister, a trompe l'œil *(see page 118).* MURALIST: COLIN FAILES;
right: a detail from a mural on a Moroccan theme in a private dining room *(see pages 82–83).* MURALIST:
STEPHEN ROBERTS; *front flap:* a decorative detail inspired by a first century A.D. Roman example. *(see page 137).* MURALIST: GARTH BENTON
Back cover: a trompe l'œil sea view mural in France *(see pages 86–87); back flap:* a trompe l'œil noticeboard *(see page 126).* MURALIST: STEPHEN ROBERTS
Page 2: a detail from a mural painted at Newfield, a country house in
northern England *(see pages 68–69).* MURALIST: GRAHAM RUST

The author and publishers have made strenuous efforts to trace the
muralists whose work is illustrated in this publication. Any inadvertent
omissions will be inserted in subsequent editions of this book.

contents

◄ **Nostalgia for the mural themes of past generations** influenced wall paintings in history, just as it does today. This misty image of a scene from an historical legend decorates a deep bay cutting into the walls of an old château. The mural, illuminated by the natural light flooding through the window, warms the cold stone walls and lightens the room's dark interior.

introduction

THIS BOOK WAS INSPIRED BY the work of the many imaginative and talented artists whose skills have transformed walls the world over. It illustrates paintings on building interiors by well-known muralists, such as the internationally acclaimed American muralist Richard Haas, and the respected British artist Graham Rust. It reproduces a few murals by famous artists, better known for their work in other media, who have occasionally expressed themselves in paintings on walls, such as the British artist David Hockney. And it illustrates works by many of the artists in this field whose murals, because they are painted on the walls of buildings, cannot easily be displayed at exhibitions and are therefore not widely known because they are rarely seen by the public.

Our aim in this book is to reveal the rich potential of murals in the widest possible range of interiors in private and public buildings – murals on the exteriors of buildings are not included. Muralists offer myriad creative ways of transforming walls, ceilings, and innumerable other surfaces with images, patterns, and colour. In houses and apartments murals can alter the apparent dimensions of any room, from attic to bedroom, living room, and basement, giving an illusion of more light and space. Murals can alter the mood and atmosphere of a room; they can emphasize attractive elements, give feature-less spaces character, and hide or disguise inferior features. Public spaces such as offices, lobbies, boardrooms, restaurants, hotels, and hospitals can all benefit from the warmth, visual stimulation, and decorative effects inge-nious muralists can achieve with paintings on walls, doors, and ceilings.

The pages of this book are filled with fascinating examples of the inter-vention of the mural in interior design. They range from simple, decorative paintings to imaginative and dramatic illusions, and from small motifs and tiny details to ambitious schemes in historic and modern buildings. The examples have been chosen to illustrate the range of mural styles and their possible visual effects. Each mural is a unique work of art whose style, content, and role in the decor are the result of a synthesis of the client's wishes and intentions with the artist's skill and imagination.

In addition to the work of living muralists, the book also illustrates some examples of murals painted in the past, for wall painting has a long history. It is, in fact, the most ancient of art forms, for paintings appeared on walls long before they were executed on canvas. Historical records of rituals, wars, victories, political events, and everyday life painted on the walls of tombs, palaces, religious buildings, and homes have left a rich heritage of mural art. Wall paintings communicate and illustrate the esthetic and ideas of bygone ages. The cave paintings that have been discovered over the last century, often in a remarkably fine state of preservation, offer what is frequently the only record of ancient art; and examples surviving from the ancient civilizations of Europe, Asia, and the Americas reveal traditions of mural painting from the first human settlements.

Among the illustrations of historic wall paintings in the book are examples from tombs, temples, and public buildings in ancient Egypt, Crete, and Etruria, and murals found in the villas and town houses of ancient Rome. Examples from later periods focus on the Renaissance, a period which saw a new momentum in wall and ceiling painting. Aspects of perspective had been known and used in the past, by Greek and Roman artists, for instance, but Renaissance architects and artists mastered and developed the principles of linear perspective. These enabled them to represent on a flat surface three-dimensional objects, such as buildings. Their understanding of perspective enabled them to represent a more realistic view of the outside world than had ever been possible before.

The Renaissance also saw the development of illusionistic painting, in which a flat wall surface could be made to apparently extend outward to vistas of city streets and squares, across landscapes and oceans to distant horizons, and ceilings could be made to open onto false views of skies and heavens. The art of what is now known universally as trompe l'œil painting was perfected during the centuries following the Renaissance, when the Baroque and Rococo styles dominated European art and architecture.

We have selected a few examples of important wall and ceiling paintings from some of these periods and movements to show how beautiful these works are; how, over the centuries, the decorative influences of one culture or historical period has influenced the development of another; and how the paintings of the past inspire contemporary interpretations and versions. We have not set out to give a historical account of wall painting, but we have briefly explained the significance of the historical murals reproduced in the book. A bibliography lists sources on the history of wall painting for anyone who wants to explore this fascinating subject.

The book begins by exploring the ideas and themes of decorative murals. These include murals featuring human figures, animals, and patterns, including plants, flowers, abstract designs, and classic ornamental designs in colours that evoke different atmospheres. There are also paintings on marine themes, murals for children, and fantasy murals.

▶ **In this outdoor scene** on a classic theme – an English fox hunt – the American muralist makes an ironic social comment. The rural setting, the horses, and their livery are all depicted in realistic detail, but the riders, in traditional English hunting dress, are foxes. This large mural, 6 feet high and 15 feet wide (1.8 metres by 4.5 metres), in acrylics on canvas, was painted for Benton's Restaurant in Tahoe, California, but now adorns the muralist's home.
MURALIST: GARTH BENTON

▲ **The wall surface treated as a blank canvas** is given a double meaning in this contemporary mural painted in an old house in Majorca, Spain. It looks like an unframed painting on a wall – but it is also a mural painted on the wall surface. It reflects the diversity of individual style and the freedom in artistic experimentation and expression that has characterized mural painting since the early 1900s.
MURALIST: FELIX DE CADENAS

The second major section of the book explores the fascinating possibilities of illusionistic paintings – trompe l'œil – which aim to trick the viewer into believing, if only for a split second, that something painted is real. Trompe l'œil murals are often created on classic themes, such as landscapes, gardens, or ocean views, intended to give an illusion of space beyond the flat wall surface, and have the effect of altering the apparent dimensions of a room. Alternatively, they may create an illusion of a shallow recess in a wall in the form of a niche, an alcove, or a bookcase. They may be surrealistic or witty. Or they may simply be a painting of any object – a vase of flowers apparently placed on a shelf, or a butterfly at rest on a wall – which, at first glance, seems real. The pages of this section are illustrated with trompe l'œil paintings on a wide variety of classic and modern themes.

The final section of the book takes a brief look at the details – motifs, designs, patterns and their elements – of which murals may be composed.

They include leaves, flowers, birds, animals, shells, neoclassical motifs – even musical instruments and fragments of pottery – exquisitely rendered in paint. For anyone planning to commission a mural for an interior, a directory at the end of the book gives details of many of the muralists whose paintings are illustrated. Under each muralist's name is an address and telephone number, and a short description of the muralist's work and areas of special interest.

This book describes and illustrates an artistic tradition that is deservedly regaining the popularity it has often held in the past. Murals are an integral part of interior design, with the power to affect and transform the appearance and atmosphere of a room in a way no other art form can. We hope it will provide ideas and inspiration for anyone searching for new and unusual ways of bringing interiors to life.

LYNETTE WRIGLEY

▲ **Pantelone flirts with Columbine** in this mural peopled with colourful stock characters from the commedia dell'arte. It was painted directly onto the walls of the entrance hall in an elegant period house, whose opulence suggested a theatrical subject. The commedia dell'arte was originally performed by travelling players in palace courtyards and village squares of the Italian states in Renaissance times.
MURALIST: BRUCE CHURCH

decorative v

wall painting

From ancient times to the present day, artists have applied paint to walls and other surfaces to create murals of stunning simplicity or imaginative complexity.

▲ **A medley of motifs** from ancient Egyptian art makes an original mural for the dining room of a private London house. The centre panel is a dreamlike trompe l'œil of Egyptian architecture.
MURALISTS: DKT

Previous page:
This dramatic pastiche of Michelangelo's Adam from the ceiling of the Sistine Chapel in the Vatican adorns a bathroom wall in the muralist's home.
MURALIST: RICHARD BAGGULEY

◄ **A procession of slaves** bearing food, tethered animals, oil, and wine is shown in this ancient Egyptian tomb painting. Stocking the tomb with all the god-king would need for his journey to the next world was part of the funerary rites. Earth pigments such as red ochre produced the reds, browns, yellows and black used in Egyptian wall painting; greens and blues were synthesized from plant dyes, copper ores and verdigris.

ANCIENT WALL PAINTINGS are a rich source of inspiration for modern muralists. Some of the artistic styles to be seen in surviving examples – many of them remarkably well preserved – have brought intriguing themes into contemporary interiors. Stylized figures can be especially effective in decorative murals and can produce strikingly dramatic images; and the figures in ancient Egyptian wall paintings, with their powerful outlines and rich colours, are especially captivating. The images in ancient Egyptian art have a particularly clear, graphic quality and are delightfully uncomplicated.

Early Egyptian wall paintings can be traced as far back as the third millennium B.C. – the late Predynastic Period. They are found mainly in tombs; they were not painted as decorations to be seen and admired but to provide resources for the tomb's occupant in the next life. The artists recorded the status the tomb owner had acquired in life and would hope to enjoy in the next, and they painted fascinating illustrations of events in the dead person's life; these, together with the accompanying hieroglyphics, told a detailed story of how he or she had lived.

Egyptian artists were generally anonymous; they worked in teams with other artist-craftsmen for their god-king, and although some became owners of tombs, and so are named and identified as artists in texts, no works of art are attributed to them.

A wall surface to be decorated was divided into registers: the lower would represent the foreground and the upper register, the background. The most important figures were represented on a huge scale; the less important figures were very much smaller. The distinctive, "twisted" pose, showing the head and legs in profile but the eye and shoulders facing forward, was the convention for depicting the human body and is characteristic of the artistic style of the ancient Egyptians: it was the artist's intention to include every detail known and understood intellectually to exist, rather than just what could be seen. So, for example, processional figures with wide shoulders and tiny waists are depicted in narrative pictures that are simple in concept, yet rich in detail.

The images in Egyptian paintings are easily identifiable and can be surprisingly easy to imitate. There is something very appealing in the stylistic simplicity of these almost childlike representations and they provide a wealth of inspirational material that may be recreated, or used as the thematic essence for a modern mural. Although many muralists draw their inspiration from the paintings in the tombs of Egyptians who died over two millennia ago, they often add their own interpretation and a twentieth-century twist.

▶ **Huge, ghostlike figures**
painted all round the walls of this
room seem to merge and
reappear as the light changes
through the day. They are
defined in bronze powder on a
background of deep indigo,
which covers walls and ceiling to
create a serene, womblike
atmosphere. An overmantel
screen by the Irish-born
designer Eileen Gray
(1879–1976) provided the
inspiration for the figures, each
of which holds stems of lotus
flowers. Entering this room – the
salon of the artist's former home,
a château in Normandy, France –
is like walking into a picture.
MURALIST: DAVID CARTER

▲ **A naked, dancing figure**
animates the wall of a New York
apartment in this mural, entitled
Caveman. The artist created
the texture of a rock surface by
lining the wall with linen and
applying a base colour on which
he painted the figure. Warm
downlighting emphasizes the
impression of movement.
MURALIST: RICHARD GILLETTE

Wall paintings surviving from a vast number of civilizations across the world
reveal a diversity of ways of painting the human form. When prehistoric cave-
dwellers began to settle and farm, from about 10,000 years ago, they
learned to paint and carve realistic, lively human figures. Throughout history,
artists the world over have demonstrated an enduring need to record the
appearance and the events in people's lives on the walls of temples, tombs,
palaces and homes, and their surviving works provide inspiration for modern
muralists guided by the same instinct.

▶ **This charming image** of a Minoan fisherman was one of several murals discovered during excavations of the ruins of the Minoan Akrotiri Palace on the Greek island of Thira (Santorini) in the Cyclades island group. The influence of the elegant figures and refined depictions of wildlife in Minoan wall paintings from the sixteenth century B.C. is frequently seen in the work of modern muralists.
NATIONAL ARCHAEOLOGICAL MUSEUM, ATHENS, GREECE

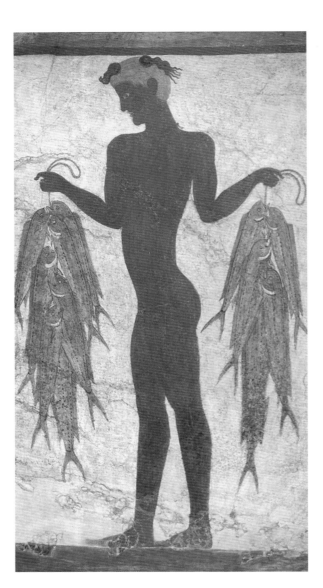

The Bronze Age culture of the seafaring Minoans on the Mediterranean island of Crete arose during the third millennium B.C. and endured until about 1400 B.C. when their great capital, Knossos, was destroyed, and their civilization declined. At the height of their development, from about 1700 B.C., they built great palaces, of which the most famous are the Palaces of Minos at Knossos and Phaístos, and sumptuous villas, which they decorated inside and out. The important rooms were adorned with figurative paintings.

Exceptionally well-preserved paintings have been discovered at the Akrotiri Palace on the island of Thira (Santorini), which was once a Minoan colony. These paintings, executed around 1550 B.C., show activities of everyday life. Such scenes also decorated the living rooms of private villas on Thira, a peaceful community of traders and fishermen. Minoan paintings show influences from the civilizations that prospered around the Mediterranean. They are similar in style to Egyptian tomb paintings, with figures in profile, but Minoan figures have a more jubilant spirit and are more carefree in style.

The Etruscans, who settled Etruria (modern Tuscany and part of Umbria) in west-central Italy around 1200 B.C., buried their dead in tombs with richly painted walls. They may have learned this art from Greek muralists, for although no tomb paintings have survived in Greece, a single Greek mural called *The Paestum Diver* was excavated in southern Italy, where the Greeks had colonies. Greek colonial artists may have developed the art and taught the Etruscans, who copied Greek traditions, techniques, and patterns in their art.

Classical traditions in Western art can be traced back to Greek art of the fifth century B.C. via the art of the Etruscans – and to the Romans, who seized power in Italy in the third century B.C. The Romans overran Etruria, but were inspired for centuries afterwards by Etruscan culture. Unlike the Etruscans, however, Romans embellished their homes with murals. Their paintings of gods and other figures on the walls of villas preserved at Pompeii and Herculaneum in southwest Italy have been recreated by many artists since their rediscovery in the 1700s and 1800s.

When Roman armies conquered Greece in the second century B.C. they plundered works of art from towns and sanctuaries. This created a demand for copies of masterpieces from the "golden age" of Greek art – the fifth century B.C. – so that Roman citizens engaged Greek artists to reproduce great classical works. Scenes containing figures, some believed to have been copied from Greek originals, were painted in panel pictures that seemed to be hung on or set into the walls of Roman town houses and country villas. For example, a mural in the Villa of Mysteries, a large country house outside Pompeii, southeast of Naples in Italy, shows figures in poses seen in Hellenic sculpture. Realistic Hellenic paintings of the human form – the nude "ideal" – became classic models on which Roman and, much later, Renaissance artists would base representations of figures.

Roman murals, which also decorated public baths and places of entertainment, encompassed diverse themes. But as Rome declined and Christianity replaced pagan religions in the Roman Empire, the quality of mural painting, the diversity of its themes, and the range of locations in which it appeared all declined. Murals were painted mainly on the ceilings of catacombs and burial vaults, generally to convey religious meaning rather than portray realistic figures.

Renaissance artists brought a tremendous revival of interest to mural painting. They broke away from the restrictions on forms imposed during the intervening Byzantine era and gave figures a new humanity. The great Florentine founders of Renaissance art, Cimabue (c. 1240–c. 1302), Giotto (c. 1266–1337), Masaccio (c. 1401–c. 1428), and Michelangelo (1475–1564), brought a new, naturalistic look to their depictions of Bible stories. Art evolved dramatically and acquired new dimensions and mastery of technique.

The religious themes and grand scale of many Renaissance frescoes may seem unsuited to the more modest demands of modern interior design. But just as Roman painters copied Greek masterpieces, and artists of the 18th and 19th century studied the elements of classical art, so have many contemporary muralists turned to Renaissance artists for inspiration. The British muralist Richard Bagguley declares himself most at home with classical themes, as is evidenced by his pastiche of a detail from Michelangelo's *Creation of Adam* reproduced on pages 12–13. And works of art are still created for great buildings. In a series of murals painted by Graham Rust for Ragley Hall in England is a magnificent ceiling depicting the temptation of Christ, which may be the largest contemporary mural ever painted.

◀ **The adventurous spirit** of the Renaissance resulted in an era of great artistic achievement in which wall painting played a major role. Writers of the time claimed that Renaissance art began with frescoes ascribed to Cimabue and those of his pupil, Giotto. This fresco in the chapel of the Palazzo Medici Riccardi, Florence, depicts the Magi arriving at Christ's nativity. The king on horseback in the foreground is said to be Lorenzo de'Medici (1449–1492), ruler of Florence and patron of the arts. ARTIST: BENOZZO GOZZOLI (c. 1421–1497)

Artists have often been commissioned by ecclesiastical or civic authorities to paint the walls and ceilings of public buildings to convey a message or to educate. In medieval Europe, for example, murals depicting Christ's life and teachings painted in churches and cathedrals had an educational role. There are many examples of wall paintings commemorating great leaders and important historical events.

In post-revolutionary Mexico, however, wall paintings with an overtly political message became the leading public art. Under President Obregón, a patron of the arts, young artists were commissioned to paint huge murals in schools and other public buildings showing scenes from Mexican history and the events of the Revolution. They were led by Diego Rivera (1866–1957), José Clemente Orozco (1883–1949), and David Sisqueiros (1896–1974), who believed that writers and artists should use their talents to support the Revolution. Many of their murals featured and glorified common people, such as the Mexican Indians and the peons (the landless peasants), who had been oppressed for centuries. Rivera claimed that for the first time Mexican mural painting made the masses the heroes of monumental art.

Rivera studied and painted in Europe between 1908 and 1921, mainly in Paris, where he knew Picasso and the Cubist painters. In Italy he studied the great Renaissance frescoes; and he exhibited in New York, where his irreverent art aroused controversy. In 1921 he returned to Mexico to join the national movement and, with Orozco and Sisqueiros, to forge a new, entirely Mexican art. Their work is now recognized as the inspiration behind the development of American mural art, as well as the monumental art of the Soviet Union and Communist China, and as the first important modern art movement outside Europe.

Rivera's aim in his painting was to combine the art of Mexico's native peoples with that of the post-colonial era. He contrasted a dwarfish Hernán Cortés, conqueror of Mexico, with the revolutionary, Emiliano Zapata, on a white horse. He painted on a monumental scale: murals he painted between 1923 and 1928 for the Ministry of Public Education in Mexico City comprised 1,997 gigantic fresco panels covering a wall area of 17,220 square feet (1,600 square metres). They are vigorous and emphatic, qualities that are considerably emphasized by the artist's bold use of flaring colours.

Rivera's fame spread rapidly and Americans soon sought his work, although they had nothing in common with him politically – in a Mexico City mural he portrayed three Americans, John D. Rockefeller, J.P. Morgan, and Henry Ford, with their wives, fashionably dressed and sipping champagne, among a number of villains.

Murals with a message are not impractical in a domestic setting and may appeal to anyone with strong views on topics of importance today. Influential people, from classical thinkers to modern folk heroes, and political themes, are just two ideas. The destruction of the rainforests, the protection of rare plants and animals, the conservation of the countryside and of folk traditions can all make excellent subjects for inspiring murals.

▲ **The Great Aztec City of Tenochtitlán** is the title of a mural painted by Diego Rivera in 1945, from which the image above is a detail. Tenochtitlán, the capital of the Aztec Empire, which at its height extended over vast areas of the Americas, was destroyed by an army of Spanish conquistadors led by Hernán Cortés in 1521, and a new capital, Mexico City, was founded on its ruins. The image depicts in exuberant colour and fine detail a scene from the city market in Plaza Tlaltelolco in Tenochtitlán. A vivacious market life is a native tradition that survived the destruction of the many civilizations that flourished in Central and South America at the time of the Spanish conquest. The central figure in the image above is a courtesan, and two figures from the crowds of indigenous Mexican peoples thronging this colourful scene can be seen in close-up in the detail on the right.

PALACIO NACIONAL, MEXICO CITY

Fish, turtles, shells, whales, and other underwater creatures have inspired art of all kinds in island and seafaring communities all over the world. They have influenced poetry and stories, legends and myths, and these have been portrayed in art over the centuries. Ancient wall paintings have been found depicting scenes and tales of the seas. For example, the art of the Minoans, who inhabited the Mediterranean island of Crete, was largely inspired by the surrounding sea. The Minoans painted underwater plants floating languidly, playful octopuses, and branching corals with a lively naturalism combined with a superb decorative sense. A painting on the walls of the Akrotiri Palace on the Greek island of Thira (Santorini), painted around 1550 B.C., shows a flotilla of boats, possibly a trading expedition, being rowed across the sea accompanied by dolphins. This mural is part of a colourful frieze of which about 18 feet (6 metres) have been preserved. It tells a visual story of life in that region of the Mediterranean as it would have been at that time.

Wall paintings survive from ancient coastal cultures in many other parts of the world. At the extreme west of the Caroline Islands in the Western Pacific is the archipelago of Belau. The work of the men of Belau's island communities has always been associated with the sea, and ships, coastal life, and marine creatures are prominent among the colourful decorations of the traditional village meeting houses of the chiefs' councils. These houses, called *bai*, some of which survive from before the coming of the Europeans in 1783, are decorated inside and out with narrative low reliefs painted in ochre pigments depicting themes ranging from myths to accounts of impor-tant events. Clam-shell icons are painted, along with other images, on the corner posts inside the *bai*, and images of ships, fish, and island life decorate the front and back façades.

The art of ancient river peoples might also serve as inspiration for modern murals. One of the best-preserved ancient Egyptian tomb-paintings, from the tomb of Nebuman at Thebes, shows the tomb-owner and his family fishing in the marshes of the Nile. Papyrus reeds, boats, fish, and underwater plants are shown in exquisite, colourful detail. And a famous eleventh-century Japanese painting entitled *Early Spring Landscape* survives on a door panel in the Byodoin Phoenix Hall in Kyoto. It shows a gently meander-ing river in early spring, with a few reeds still covered in snow.

Natural themes can have great appeal for people living in modern cities. The blues and greens that dominate aquascapes are relaxing colours – shades of aquamarine and turquoise evoke shallow, warm, sunny waters, and soft shades of blue create a tranquil atmosphere.

A bathroom is the obvious choice for a mural on a marine theme, but any utilitarian room with only plain and immobile features can be revitalized with an imaginative painting on any theme. Images do not need to be painted on a large or imposing scale to be effective, nor do they have to be elaborate to be dramatic. Sea creatures such as octopuses with swaying tentacles, or reef fish with their extraordinary shapes and spectral colours, can make delightful small images for the walls of a bathroom or a child's bedroom or nursery.

▲ **In the hands** of a skilful artist a plain bathroom seems to have taken a voyage to the bottom of the sea. The muralist decorated the walls with a scene of a coral reef, and painted sun-dappled ripples on the ceiling so that it looks like the ocean surface, seen from below. A trompe l'œil disguises a bathroom cabinet as a submersible, and a utilitarian shower curtain rail looks like a submarine companionway.
MURALIST: MINT

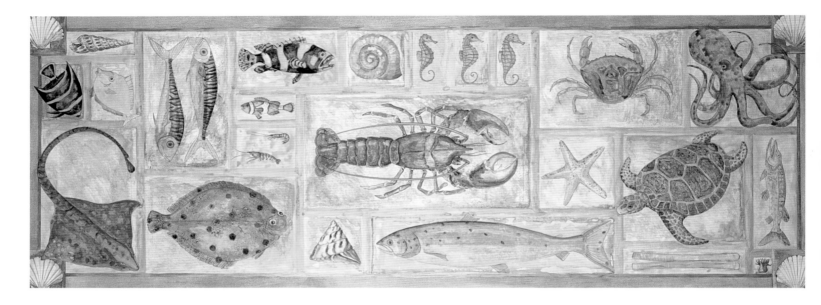

▲ Diverse sea creatures of different shapes and sizes made a perfect design to fit along the upper part of a sloping kitchen wall, in an awkward space just above eye level. The mural – a wedding present for the artist's sister, a cook – is painted in acrylics and varnished to protect it from the steam and heat of the kitchen.
MURALIST: REBECCA CAMPBELL

Superb close-up photographs of marine life forms can be found in books and magazines, and films show undersea life in motion. These sources provide an accessible and inexhaustible catalogue of forms and patterns for muralists to study for inspiration. The simple shapes and colourful patterns of fish, the extraordinary diversity of invertebrate life, and the brilliant colours of corals and sponges can hardly fail t stimulate the imagination of any artist, professional or amateur.

Edible sea creatures – a crab, a lobster, a turtle, and fish commonly used in cooking – were the main theme of the kitchen mural by London artist Rebecca Campbell, reproduced above. Campbell trained as an illustrator, but in the 1990s she began to paint murals and furniture. Her work on a series of designs for trays gave her the idea of a mural composed of sea creatures, each painted inside a roughly square or oblong shape and assembled like a jigsaw puzzle into a rectangular mural which could be fitted into the restricted space available on a wall above kitchen fittings. The artist has since reproduced this successful design as wrapping paper.

Shells were an important decorative motif in the Rococo style of interior decoration that became popular in Europe in the 1700s. The scrolls, the c- and s-curves, and the rhythmic, flowing movement that are characteristic of the style were derived from marine life. Toward the 1800s, decorations composed of seashells arranged in patterns were sometimes applied to whole wall surfaces, particularly in grottoes.

Shells are a favourite natural motif of the English muralist Graham Rust, whose work is recognized internationally. He frequently uses them in decorative panels and screens "because they are such attractive and varied objects". They often appear in his larger trompe l'œil murals in painted, sculptural forms.

The fantastic, larger-than-life mural of gigantic shells and starfish by Robert O'Dea, reproduced above, creates a stunning, dramatic impact in a hotel restaurant in Tel Aviv, Israel. The gentle curves and outlines tumble across the wall, rich in textural detail, and the warm tones of the soft colours blend and harmonize with the decor of the restaurant.

The artist painted this mural directly onto the restaurant wall, but murals painted for public places, such as hotels and offices, are usually painted on canvas or board in the artist's studio, to be transported to their location when they are finished and then attached to the wall. Canvas panels can be rolled up for transportation and retouched, where necessary, when they are in place. This is often the only way of producing a mural for a busy public place, which may close only for a few hours in a week. A large-scale work might involve many weeks of preparation and painting, which would be impossible to carry out in the bustle of a commercial site.

Rebecca Campbell finds painting onto a panel in her studio the most comfortable and workable solution for herself and her clients – many of whom ask for their mural to be painted in this way in case they want to move it to another room, or in anticipation of the day they next move house.

▲ **Seashells and starfish** of Israel's Mediterranean coast were the inspiration for this mural, which stretches across the 33-foot (10-metre) width of the main restaurant of Radisson Moriah Hotel in Tel Aviv. Fascinated by the surface details of marine invertebrates, the muralist decided to focus not on their shape so much as their surface texture. His mural represents shellfish and starfish on an unusual scale – as if they were being looked at through a magnifying lens.
MURALIST: ROBERT O'DEA

▶ **The light, elegant style** of the Georgian architect Robert Adam was influential in Britain into the early 1800s. His studies of Roman art led him to develop a delicate, flowing style of architecture and interior design. He rebuilt the façade of a Tudor mansion, Osterley Park outside London, and redecorated the interior. This illustration shows the Etruscan Room – so called because the painted motifs and medallions resembled the designs on Greek pots, which were thought at the time to be Etruscan. Stucco reliefs in the terracotta tone of Greek vases also decorate the walls and ceiling of Adam's Etruscan rooms in English country mansions.
MURALIST: ROBERT ADAM

▶ **This detail** from Robert Adam's Etruscan Room at Osterley shows a figurative group positioned above the mantelpiece, delicately tinted in terracotta. Classical ornamental motifs such as this were copied into pattern books for use by future architects and decorators. Today, they are still used by interior designers and muralists as source material for elegant wall decorations for both period and modern houses – a tribute to the enduring elegance of classical and neoclassical design.

The excavation of the buried Roman towns at Pompeii and Herculaneum, which began in 1748, had a stimulating effect on art and architecture in Europe. Renaissance artists had looked into history to find inspiration in the art of antiquity, but after 1748 artists could physically study works by their classical forebears. A new – neoclassical – style emerged, which embraced the restraint and sobriety of classical art. It was partly a reaction against the excesses of the stylistic movements that preceded it: the dramatic grandeur of the Baroque; the elaborate fantasy of the Rococo; Palladian severity.

Neoclassical style is characterized by a formality achieved by the use of geometric forms and the economical use of Greek and Roman architectural adornment – columns, pilasters, pediments, and friezes. Fresco became an essential component of interior design – in the Italian states, where the new style began, frescoes covered walls and ceilings of palaces and villas.

European artists and architects visited Pompeii and Herculaneum in the 1700s and spread classical ideas through sketches and paintings. Neoclassicism took hold in France, Russia, and in Britain particularly. The Scottish architect Robert Adam (1728–92), captivated by the lighthearted charm of Pompeian art, designed graceful façades and delicate interiors that were a departure from the monumental Palladian style which preceded them in Britain.

▲ **Stencilled flowers** and leaves, panels framed with floral borders, and pretty swags, their shape echoing that of the painted plant forms, create visual interest without darkening a rather dim hall. This pretty painting in soft pastel colours on a light background recalls Robert Adam's neoclassical decorations of the 1700s in English houses and gives a similar impression of studied elegance.
MURALIST: GEORGE OAKES

Leaf and flower motifs make attractive decorations. They may be painted as formal, controlled patterns or as a riotous profusion exploding over a wall. The exuberant Rococo style of interior decoration, which developed in France in the 1700s, incorporated designs derived from nature in which curving organic forms were assembled into delicate patterns.

Plants are an easy natural theme to live with. Formal arrangements of naturalistic motifs designed as separate but harmonious groups make a useful decorative device with which to integrate wall panels and embellish bare wall surfaces, and random designs of climbing foliage give a casual but uniform effect.

Climbing and trailing plants can be worked into a pretty design with which to decorate small areas of wall. These versatile motifs are particularly useful for enlivening narrow walls, such as the end walls of corridors and hallways, and integrating them with the walls on either side by extending spiralling tendrils across them onto the adjoining surfaces. A decorative mural like this is intended to be seen as a pattern on a wall (unlike a trompe l'œil, which creates an illusion of space beyond it). If, however, it is painted with a high degree of realism and attention to proportion, it may be described as a surface trompe l'œil. Murals painted to look like old tapestries, which were popular during the 1500s and 1600s, are a good example of this.

▲ **Trelliswork** entwined with a trailing ivy with tendrils that twist and turn has been used to make a flat, dull wall at the end of a passage eye-catching. The symmetry of the trellis is echoed by the design of the occasional table and the placing of objects upon it; and any tendency to monotony is subtly relieved by the ivy's meanderings, which draw the eye toward the central motif, of which the candelabra forms an integral part.

◀ **These luxurious wall decorations** adorn the ladies' powder room of Radio City Music Hall in Rockefeller Center, New York City. They were painted around 1930. During the Depression years President Roosevelt initiated a mural program for out-of-work artists, extending a fashion in America for murals that stemmed from the influence of the Mexican muralist Diego Rivera. In all periods of history, plants have proved appropriate mural subjects. Here, huge green leaves complement the warm tones of the beautifully paint-washed walls.

MURALIST: YASUO KUNIYOSHI

▲ **This antique narrative woodblock wallpaper** is one of only four surviving examples by the French brothers DuFour, printed in 1815 and entitled "The Voyages of Captain Cook". It was recently bought at auction by Mr. and Mrs. Hoffman of Palm Springs, California, to be pasted in their private dining room, and they commissioned the distinguished American muralist to add a 2-foot (0.6-metre) strip along the top of the section shown in the illustration above. The artist glued canvas to the wall and painted directly onto it, using acrylics and matching the colours visually.

MURALIST: GARTH BENTON

▲ **This trompe l'œil figure** –
one of the characters in the
section of wallpaper shown
opposite – was painted on the
door leading from the clients'
dining room into their kitchen.
The muralist has depicted him
as a server carrying a basket of
exotic fruit. The pilasters and
the motif over the door are also
trompe l'œil images, painted in
acrylics on canvas and glued to
the wall. The wallpaper sample
did not reach all the way round
the room, and the sections on
either side of this door – 10 feet
(3.5 metres) to the left and 1
foot (0.35 metres) to the right –
were added by the artist.
MURALIST: GARTH BENTON

Flowers and plants have always been a feature of murals and trompe l'œil.
They have provided designs and motifs for generations of artists stretching
back to the ancient Egyptians, who illustrated plants in their tomb paintings,
commonly depicting papyrus grass and lotus flowers. They are found in
friezes decorating the homes of officials and nobles, and in palace decorations. The powerful outlines and colourful, stylized flowers of Egyptian art
translate easily onto the walls of contemporary homes.

Wall paintings from later periods are more natural. One of the earliest
Minoan frescoes so far discovered is a lovely painting from a villa at Amnisos
near Knossos in Crete, painted around 1600 B.C. It shows three tall, white
lilies growing from their calyx of green leaves and illustrates how Cretan
artists combined observation of nature with a decorative flair.

Nature was a popular theme in Roman wall paintings. A mural from the
Villa Livia outside Rome (see page 65), executed late in the first century B.C.,
is typical of garden scenes that were often painted on the walls of larger,
more luxurious villas and palaces. Its wild garden full of graceful trees and
birds, believed to have belonged to Livia, wife of the Emperor Augustus, has
inspired some contemporary interpretations.

The work of past generations of painters, architects, and designers
provides the inspiration for the paintings of many modern muralists.
Recreating historical periods in works of art is one of the specialities of Garth
Benton, the American muralist from California. In his twenties, he was so
transfixed by the scale, execution and sheer beauty of a wall painting in the
style of the Italian artist Giambattista Tiepolo (1696–1770), that he decided
to make mural painting his life's work. Today he has an impressive client list
and is renowned for his ability to tackle a wide diversity of styles and themes:
Pompeii, French Rococo, a Chinese mandarin's garden, an English hunt, and
many others. He has also restored damaged sections of two of only four
surviving samples of the antique American wallpaper reproduced opposite.
Benton immerses himself in the culture and art history of the period before
beginning work on a commission.

Murals are known to have influenced wallpaper design – and vice versa.
Wallpaper, believed to have been devised as an inexpensive substitute for
tapestry, was in use in England and France by the late 1400s. By the early
1700s its use was flourishing. Flower patterns and chinoiserie became
popular, and soon hand-painted wallpapers were being imported from China.
Artists began copying the delicately coloured designs they saw on oriental
wallpaper, painting Chinese landscapes with pagodas and stunted trees on walls.

By the late 1700s the leaders of contemporary design were French, and
scenic wallpapers decorated with landscapes evolved in France. This trend
was followed in the 1800s by a preference for wallpapers illustrating historical
themes, derived, perhaps, from the influence of recently excavated murals of
that period. Later in the century there was a vogue for repetitive patterns –
of flowers particularly – in England and France. The wallpaper designs of the
English designer William Morris (1834–96) followed this tradition.

▲ **The mosaiclike paintings** of Gustav Klimt inspired this mural painted for Oscar's Restaurant, London. The panels present a wonderful expanse of colour, and abstract shapes composed of layers of texture suggest movement. This is heightened by the mirrors and the halogen downlighting, which makes the metallic pigments sparkle.
MURALIST: ROBERT O'DEA

Western art of the early 1900s was characterized by a new freedom in artistic experimentation. The result was a great diversification of themes and styles, many of which were incorporated in murals. The concept of abstract art (the idea that shapes and colours can convey meanings and esthetic values independently of figurative and other subjects) gained favour with many artists as the century progressed. The idea was not new – geometric and other abstract patterns had been used in decoration, notably in Moslem religious buildings, for many centuries – but it was given a new lease of life in new movements in art and by notable artists of the time. Outstanding among

◄ **This detail from a panel** shows the variety of techniques, including painting, stippling and stencilling, used to recreate the abstract forms and shimmering colour in the paintings of Gustav Klimt. The British muralist, Robert O'Dea, was briefed to research the Klimt oeuvre, but to use no figures. He achieved the effects using acrylic colours with gold, silver, and bronze powders in glazes. The panels, each 9 feet high and 3 feet wide (3 metres by 1 metre), with a large panel 9 feet by 2 feet (3 metres by 1.8 metres), were painted in the artist's studio.
MURALIST: ROBERT O'DEA

them was Gustav Klimt (1862–1918). An Austrian painter and designer who worked mainly on architectural decoration, Klimt was a strong influence in Austrian decorative arts during the 1800s and early 1900s. He was associated with the Symbolist movement, which was based on the idea that art should concern itself with suggestion through symbolic images. Abstract art permits limitless freedom of expression and has been used to create extraordinary murals. Patterns may be composed of unusual and original shapes and colour combinations which, especially when painted on all the walls of a room, may seem to make them move or shimmer.

◀ **The colours used in a mural** influence a room's mood, and an abstract mural is a perfect medium for colour, unleashing its emotional power. Blues are the basis of this unusual bathroom scheme. The zigzag shapes in indigo and white check the soporific effect a monochrome background might have. Complementary scarlet for a drape and other details results in a pleasing balance of primary hues.
MURALIST: MICK HURD

▲ **A spiral design** in gold and terracotta makes this bathroom, inspired by the work of Gustav Klimt and designed by the muralist for his Normandy château, glow with warm colour through cold winters. Stencils were made for the Mycenaen spirals, through which the acrylic base colour was applied, and the connecting lines were drawn freehand. Gold powders in a gold base plus acrylic glazes produce the glow.
MURALIST: DAVID CARTER

▶ **An elegant chinoiserie** mural runs all round the walls of this oval foyer. Painted in soft blues and greens and warm ochres and siennas, it makes an inviting entrance to this palatial home in Palm Springs, California. The artist drew on a multiplicity of sources – from the works of the great Chinese painters to an old Chinese calendar (for the pagodas), botanical drawings, and photographs of oriental bird species. He painted the mural in acrylics on canvas panels 54 inches (137 centimetres) wide. These were rolled up for delivery to the site, pasted onto the wall like wallpaper, then retouched.
MURALIST: GARTH BENTON

The artistic expression of the modern muralist has its origins in the art of prehistoric people, whose creative work, produced without the aid of modern technology or inspiration from any more ancient artistic style, has been found on the walls of caves in Australia, Europe, Africa, America, and many other parts of the world.

Many modern artists have been influenced by the spirit and vitality in cave painting. The most celebrated examples of this ancient artform are the paintings of animals in the caves at Altamira in northern Spain and Lascaux in the Dordogne in France. These representations of bison, mammoths, sabre-toothed tigers, deer, and horses have such remarkably lifelike forms and naturalistic expression that after the discovery of Altamira in 1879 most archeologists declared the paintings fakes. Only after 1940, when still more vivid paintings were found at Lascaux, was their antiquity confirmed: these caves are thought to have been painted about 15,000 years ago. Cave art seems to have survived up to perhaps 5,000 years ago in Europe, but it continued until a much later date among the Native Americans, the Australian Aborigines, and the South African Bushmen.

Prehistoric artists used the naturally occurring pigments in minerals. Their reds, yellows, and browns came from ochre and hematite; and their dark browns and violets from types of manganese. These minerals were ground into a fine powder and applied to damp limestone walls and ceilings with fingers and also with brushes made from fur, pads of moss, sticks, and feathers. Outlines were sometimes filled in by spraying or blowing the powder colours onto the rock through tubular bones.

Archeologists surmise that some paintings may have been placed deliberately on irregularities of the rock surfaces in order to highlight the curves and contours of the back or belly of an animal. Working in the dim illumination of primitive candles among the dark shadows of the caves, the imagined images of these animals may have inspired the cave artists, just as we see forms in the moving shadows thrown on walls by flickering lights. Unaccountably, the animals represented in cave art are not always the species that prehistoric people normally hunted and ate; and some paintings have been found in dark, inaccessible recesses deep within certain caves where people did not live. This seems to suggest that the paintings were not decorative, but may have been created for ritualistic or magical purposes.

Modern muralists often depict animals in natural or stylized ways. But today they are most likely to seek a smooth, sound, flat, uninterrupted wall surface, which they prepare with a base of emulsion paint before painting the mural using acrylics or oil paints and a wide selection of brushes. A modern wall is also likely to have inconveniently positioned wall sockets and light switches, radiators, and other electrical devices with which the muralist must contend. Fortunately such obstructions can often be incorporated into a mural as successfully as the cave artists made use of irregular rock faces. Windows, doors and fireplaces which interrupt a wall surface should be considered and incorporated into the design at the planning stage.

◄ **The rustic quality** of this mural is achieved by combining paintings of a domestic goat and local plants in an impressionist style. The mural is one of several painted on the walls of the farmhouse on a 1,000-year-old *finca* or estate farm near Campanet on the island of Majorca, Spain. The proprietor briefed a local artist to paint anything he could see from the windows, and the result is a series of vignettes of rural life in the Balearic Islands. The mural extends across the wall of the room and surrounds the door, which does not disrupt the image or disturb its effect.
MURALIST: FELIX DE CADENAS

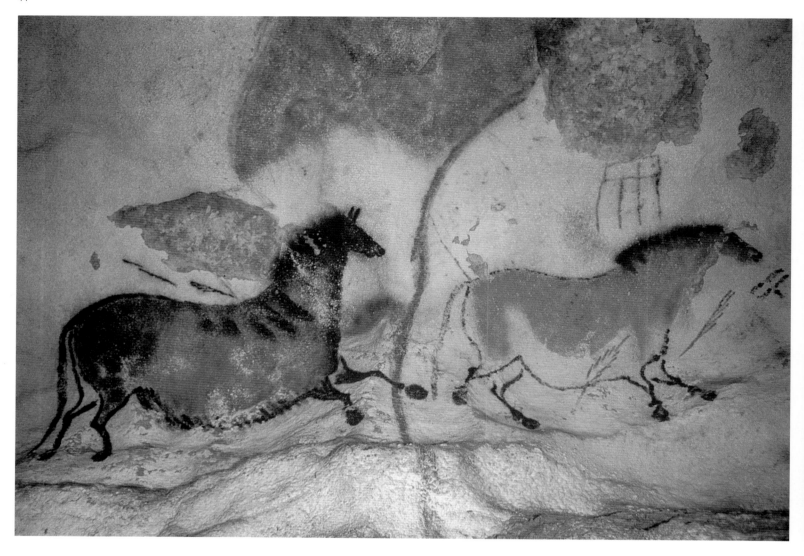

▲ **These two splendid horses** were painted in black, yellow, brown, and red earth colours on the wall of a gallery in the caves at Lascaux, France, by nomadic hunter-gatherers perhaps 15,000 to 20,000 years ago. Carbon dioxide breathed into the cave atmosphere by visitors is fading the ancient colours, so the paintings were copied onto the walls of a replica cave nearby for visitors to see, and the original cave closed. The mysterious atmosphere of cave paintings like these is occasionally captured in murals by artists today.

Animals appear to have been the major theme of prehistoric artists the world over. They seem rarely to have depicted human figures, and in those discovered so far their figures often look like stickmen or the unsophisticated drawings of small children. Their representations of people do not have the degree of realism and movement they achieved in their magnificent bison, horses, and other animals. They occasionally painted what appear to be female fertility symbols and other strange symbols, as yet unidentified, and they left imprints of hands on cave walls, but no images of plants, trees, or landscapes have been found.

Animated human forms began to appear when nomadic hunters became settlers and farmers. The transitional period seems to have been about 6000 B.C., the date of a wall painting found in the earliest known settlement: Çatal Hüyük in southern Anatolia, Turkey, which is believed to be the earliest painting on the plaster-washed walls of a domestic house. The human figures in this wall painting are more animated than in any earlier art that has so far been discovered, and they consequently have a lifelike quality.

▲ **This gorilla** is one animal in a mural depicting creatures in their habitats painted on the walls of Café Dodo in the zoo on the island of Jersey, off the coast of southern England. As it progresses around the café's seating area the mural moves around the world and through the day – the gorilla is shown in tropical Africa in mid-afternoon. Jersey Zoo is famous for its family of gorillas and its orangutans, who are depicted most prominently. The mural was painted in oils directly onto a prepared satinwood surface, and varnished for protection.
MURALIST: CATHERINE PERRYMAN

Nowadays, murals may depict commonly seen creatures or illustrate more exotic animals from films and photographs. The nursery, playroom or a child's bedroom are the most likely rooms in the house to have colourful animal paintings on the walls. They may depict a child's favourite cartoon characters, or small animals, such as Beatrix Potter rabbits, might be painted in muted tones to create a mural for toddlers.

It is relatively easy to paint a children's animal mural. An image can be painted in outline, then filled in. Giraffes might extend right up to the ceiling and amusing monkeys can be painted swinging across the walls. Elephants with curving trunks and huge ears might move along a skirting board, and tigers and leopards can stalk through thick jungles, peering out from a vivid background of tropical foliage.

Not all children will want animals to look anthropomorphic or amusing. Older children may prefer a mural of real animals in their habitats – even threatened species they are unlikely ever to see, but might want to help preserve by deepening their knowledge and understanding of them.

▲ **Images of animals** can be perfect subjects for paintings of unusual shapes and sizes. The animals and birds of the African plains were chosen for this unusual screen painting. Each wooden panel is 6 feet high and 18 inches wide (1.8 metres by 50 centimetres).
MURALIST: JAYNE POPE

A mural can transport the viewer into a dream landscape – a vista across the Tuscan countryside, over a desert to the distant horizon, or to a tropical island far away in a blue sea. Everyone has a favourite place or time to which they dream of escaping – which may be why fantasies of foreign lands, with their associated colours and textures, are such a popular theme for murals.

Sources of ideas for murals depicting foreign places are all around us. Eastern fabric designs – the colours and patterns picked from saris, kabayas, sarongs, and other garments, or from cushions, rugs, and bedspreads can inspire decorative themes for panels on walls or on furniture. Carved boxes, inlaid tables, mandalas, ancient scriptures, and traditional block prints can all be a source of decorative motifs to paint in a frieze, with touches of gold for oriental opulence. From Iceland to Australia, Chile to Japan, every country has its historic culture, traditional artefacts, and folk or classic art, which might inspire a mural. Museums and libraries have decorated objects, prints, paintings, and books to consult for ideas and inspiration.

Josephine Lely, a British muralist, turned a dream into reality when she set out to find work in the Caribbean. She was soon busy painting bright, colourful murals on the walls of restaurants and bars. Her first commission, for a restaurant, was the tropical underwater fantasy illustrated below. For reference sources she scoured magazines for pictures of marine life of the Caribbean Sea, but it was not long before she was inspired to learn to scuba dive and to investigate the atmosphere and colours of the sea for herself.

▼ **The vivid colours** of corals and sponges on the Caribbean reefs are captured in this fantasy undersea mural for a Barbados restaurant. A romantic wreck and the strange shapes of tube worms, reef octopus, and other sea life, are all given a cartoon style treatment. But native fish such as the great barracuda are accurately portrayed, testifying to the artist's careful observations on a series of diving trips. She painted on canvas stretched across a floor. Because of the humid atmosphere, a drying medium was added to the oils. The painted canvas was attached to battens nailed to the restaurant wall.
MURALIST: JOSEPHINE LELY

Over the five years she spent painting on the Caribbean islands, Lely's mural style changed. At home she had painted traditional English gardens on a small scale. Painting on a large scale can be an exciting, challenging experience for a muralist, and in the tropics, faced with attempting to reproduce the brilliant colours of her surroundings on larger wall surfaces, she began painting light-hearted scenes of life in the Caribbean, some depicting amusing cartoon-style characters.

There are no limits to the visions an artist can realize in a mural. In one example, a client who often visited Morocco wanted the British muralist, Bruce Church, to create a North African atmosphere in her London home. Along the bottom of the designated wall the artist painted tiles in a Moroccan design. Above them he painted a desert scene of Bedouins and their camels, using reddish browns and other earth colours, then distressing the walls when the painting was finished.

When commissioning a mural, a client often asks an artist to suggest a theme. In recent years, however, it has become increasingly common for people to plan their own interior design themes when decorating their homes, and a theme for a mural will often occur to a client as part of the scheme for the decor. Formulating the initial idea for a mural can unlock the creativity hiding in everyone. Discussing the painting and working out the details with a muralist are part of the creative process, and also provide a satisfying outlet for individual self-expression.

The Romans painted mythological scenes in different rooms in their houses: each living room was under the protection of a different deity; Bacchus might be represented in the dining room and Venus in a bedroom. Even today, traditional subjects such as Roman myths and deities and figures and scenes from classical literature are always popular themes for murals, and artists who can create them are much sought after.

The imagination can create fabulous murals from any idea, from the past or the present. However, amateur artists often find it easier and more rewarding to paint a subject from the imagination than a classical composition involving realistic representation and perspective, for which some training in technical and artistic skills is needed.

When a restaurateur commissioned the British muralist Robert O'Dea to paint a series of murals for his Japanese restaurant in London, he asked the artist to paint one panel in traditional Japanese style to conform with the restaurant's decor, but to make the illustration surprising in some way. After considering a number of ideas they agreed on a landscape – a traditional theme in Japanese painting. O'Dea chose a view across a mountain range with clouds and mist swirling around the peaks. But by clever use of bright colours he has succeeded in giving the landscape a surprise element: the mountain peaks look like the crests of waves and they are coloured with ocean blues; this landscape looks more like a seascape. In its theme and its colouring it evokes the famous painting *Fuji Seen Through The Waves Off Kanagawa* by the Japanese artist, Katsushika Hokusai (1760–1849). It also gives a mystical impression, recalling the rich tradition of Japanese myths and legends of the sea.

O'Dea is an artist of wide experience, having studied textile print design and worked in several design studios in the course of his career, including Liberty's store in London, and his murals are always beautifully coloured. He is also a photographer, a skill he uses as a method of research and reference for his murals. His work is widely published in travel magazines, and he consequently travels to carry out his photographic commissions. Foreign travel clearly influences his painting, providing constant inspiration and visual ideas on which to draw for themes for his murals, and it facilitates his work with a number of international clients.

▶ **A Japanese landscape** with the dreamy quality of the classic style, but with more colour, in keeping with the decor, was the brief for this mural for a new branch of the Benihana restaurant chain in London. After studying the work of the great Japanese masters, the artist decided on this view of mountains heavily shrouded in mist. He painted the scene in oil paints and glazes and used gold leaf and copper leaf to line the hillsides. A large mural, 13 feet high by 50 feet long (4 metres by 12 metres), it was painted directly onto the restaurant wall. The muralist took advantage of the existing downlighting to highlight the peaks and pick up the reflection from the metallic pigments.
MURALIST: ROBERT O'DEA

Decorative murals are especially welcome and cheerful additions to the unglamorous, clinical environments of hospitals. Such institutional buildings, whose architecture is often harsh and unsympathetic, can benefit from a mural, which will make the environment less austere and impersonal. Murals are often commissioned to cheer up receptions, waiting rooms, and other public areas, but they can be far more effective in a ward. Research has shown that a pleasing environment can hasten the recovery of patients from surgery; and in a children's ward the colours, stories and humour a mural can provide can radically reduce the sense of alienation and stress that is often felt by young patients in hospital.

The image from a mural shown on this page was painted for the young inhabitants of the children's isolation ward of the Royal Darwin Hospital in the Northern Territory of Australia. Nurses working on this fifth-floor ward in a high-rise building, aided by administrative and other medical staff, raised the money for the commission. They wanted to enliven the high-tech ward environment and heighten its comfort for their patients, ninety per cent of whom are Aboriginal and normally live far from towns and cities.

Painstaking consultations between the muralists, Gavin Wrigley and Martin Selwood of Street-Level Public Art, the staff, and the hospital board, taking cultural references, images and their associations, and colour therapy into consideration, resulted in a brightly coloured Rainbow Serpent winding its way around 147 feet (45 metres) of ward walls. In Aboriginal mythology the Rainbow Serpent is the creator of landforms. In its journey across this children's ward, the Rainbow Serpent unifies painted landscapes of Australia's Northern Territory, beginning at an image of arid desert, progressing through painted scrub and open woodland to monsoon forest, winding through escarpment country to the coast, and finally submerging itself beneath the northern oceans. The ward is open-plan in concept, but divided by glass partitions, so images in one area can be seen from others.

The muralists commissioned Aboriginal artists to paint some of the images, and a flow of ideas developed in which photorealism mingled with stylized Aboriginal images. Aboriginal art is thought to have originated more than 30,000 years ago – in the era when the earliest rock paintings are thought to have been made. The religious beliefs of the Aborigines focus on the ancestors and on mythical animals who are believed to have created the world. Although much of their culture was destroyed by European settlement on the Australian continent, the Aborigines have preserved, unbroken over centuries, a rich oral tradition of myths relating the time of the ancestors, called "The Dreaming" to the present. Their ancient rituals – which they continue to practise – are intended to preserve the flow of life.

Characters from folk tales and myths make wonderful decorations in children's bedrooms and nurseries, as well as in public buildings. For inspiration, turn to children's books, for many have pages of delightful illustrations from which theme ideas may be drawn. Favourite characters from modern stories are familiar "friends" to bring a child daily delight.

▲ **Turtles at a billabong,** by two Aboriginal artists is a section of the Rainbow Serpent mural in the Isolated Children's Ward of Royal Darwin Hospital in northern Australia. The two muralists laid down a background theme of bright colours using spray guns and splatter techniques with occasional brushstrokes, and the Aboriginal artists added striking images.

Like these turtles at a creek, these images all evoke natural life in the ancient lands of Australia's Northern Territory, a centre of Aboriginal culture. Four artists took fourteen weeks to execute this complex work.
MURALISTS: GAVIN WRIGLEY AND MARTIN SELWOOD
ARTISTS: MARTINA PARRY YILIMU (BACKGROUND) AND MARJORIE MORGAN (TURTLES)

▲ **The circus theme** for this children's mural in a London house was suggested by the room's stripy curtains. Bright primary colours appeal to all children, and here the artist has used them in varied patterns of squares, stripes, and stars. The mural is full of things to look at – circus animals, traditional circus characters, such as stilt walkers and clowns, and a performance in full swing in the Big Top. The artist painted the scene in her studio in acrylics on panels of MDF board. The panels were cut to the shapes of the tops of the tents – which follow the shapes of the wall lights. At its highest point the mural is 5 feet 2 inches (1.55 metres) and it runs 12 feet (3.6 metres) along the children's bedroom wall.
MURALIST: REBECCA CAMPBELL

When planning a mural for a child's room, always consult the child and choose a theme that is not too haunting. A mural can project a powerful image. Children have occasionally been so overawed by an image chosen by their parents that they have had to change rooms. It may be obvious that pictures of goblins, devils, and wolves should not appear on the walls of young children's bedrooms, but some apparently innocuous images can be disturbing. Patterns in complementary colours that dazzle when juxtaposed – red and green, bright blue and vivid orange, and yellow and purple, and the Op Art effects of moiré patterns in black and white – might have the effect of making children feel giddy.

Two lucky London children wake up each morning to the enchanting scenes of circus tents, clowns, and trapeze artists in the mural above, painted by Rebecca Campbell. Another magical mural in this artist's repertoire of children's murals is a scene of hills and winding roads with distant villages, sea shores, sailing ships, and brightly coloured hot air balloons. Dragons and fairy tale figures gaze at the view.

◀ **A striking wooden screen** has been beautifully decorated with colourful paintings inspired by the art of Mogul India. The tallest panel is 6 feet high and 18 inches wide (1.8 metres by 50 centimetres). The wooden frames of all three panels are gilded – like Indian paintings of the Mogul period (1526–1857), and they are embedded with a mosaic composed of fragments of broken glass in colours echoing those in the paintings.
MURALIST: JAYNE POPE

A screen may be thought of both as a portable wall and as a versatile piece of furniture. In its role as a temporary wall, a screen may be a room divider, creating intimate areas within it; or it may conceal an essential but unattractive object or feature. Yet a superbly carved or elegantly shaped screen also has a role as a decorative item of furniture, and a beautifully painted screen can be a stunning feature in a room, as effective as a picture or a mural.

Many muralists paint furniture as well as walls. They can transform old chests or chests of drawers with a painting, or make a cupboard or a wardrobe disappear into a wall by painting part of a mural across it (see pages 126–131). A painted table can add visual interest to a room on the horizontal plane. Small-scale decorative features such as painted screens and furniture can look charming when appropriately positioned in a room, contributing an element of spontaneity to interior decoration.

Paintwork need not be loud or invasive to be effective. An alcove, a niche, the wall behind a shelving unit are all ideal locations for simple painted decorations that will not overwhelm a room.

▶ **A secret door** in a secluded corner of a London architect's apartment in the city's Docklands area has been cleverly hidden with a mural after the style of artist Mark Rothko (1903–70). The artist studied the Rothko oeuvre and composed the mural from eight works with tonal similarities. The rectangular panels with their blended colours fit the irregular space perfectly. The mural also lends character to this recessed corner framed by the room's wooden architecture.
MURALIST: ROBERT O'DEA

A good muralist does not always have to cover a whole wall or ceiling with colour to create a planned effect, but can often achieve it by painting a surprisingly small area. The smallest of homes may have an unsightly space begging to be disguised by a decorative mural. A plain doorway, for example, may be turned into a distinguished entrance with the addition of an appropriate mural. A colourful, playful theme may answer the problem of how to disguise a boarded-up doorway in a house that has been converted into apartments, what to do about the awkwardly shaped doors of an under-stair cupboard, or how to treat an uninteresting entrance to a basement.

The mural above is one of several transformations of uninteresting entranceways in public buildings by the American muralist, Richard Haas. This respected artist brings a problem-solving element to his work, which, in another example – not illustrated here – inspired him to transform the glass-panelled lobby doors of a financial institution in Phoenix, Arizona, into a grand entrance by surrounding them with a mural on a Native American theme.

In the mural on the left, a secret door leading into a hidden room has been perfectly concealed beneath a mural, which also redefines the irregularly shaped corner of a room. Small, asymmetrical wall spaces and recesses like this might look cluttered if hung with a framed picture, but they can be perfect sites for a mural. There are many examples of inventive murals cleverly designed to fit wildly irregular spaces.

▲ **An imaginative mural** transforms the stark, rather clinical appearance of these doors at the entrance to the subterranean dining area in the New York headquarters of the Philip Morris Company. Without the mural that frames them they looked cold and featureless; with it they seem welcoming: the red-coated figures of the bellboys seem to invite the executives to pass through them into the dining room on the other side.
MURALIST: RICHARD HAAS

trompe l'œil

and illusion

By definition, trompe l'œil
is something that deceives
the eye, a clever trick of
artistic deception used to
create a false impression
of space and perspective.

WITH THE SKILFUL USE of perspective, careful detailing of life-size objects, and contrasts of light and shade, an artist can paint a mural that is not only decorative but also plays on the senses, persuading us to believe – if only for an instant – that what is painted is real. This is trompe l'œil, a French term meaning "fool the eye".

Technically, trompe l'œil in mural painting is the illusion created when an artist paints a three-dimensional picture on a two-dimensional surface, intending to alter the viewer's perception of the flat wall surface. Unlike a framed picture, in which the three-dimensional effect is contained within the frame, a trompe l'œil mural embraces an entire object or scene, immersing the onlooker in a fantasy vision of a distant garden, a rolling landscape, a sea view, or roads disappearing toward a horizon.

The illusion is enhanced when the artist integrates the composition sympathetically and imaginatively with its surroundings. A trompe l'œil mural might cover an entire wall, or more than one wall. Alternatively, it might be just a detail on a surface where such an object might be expected to appear – a painted fire surround, for example, over a real fireplace, on which is displayed in life-size detail different objects that usually collect there, such as a clock, candles, photographs, and a vase of flowers.

Trompe l'œil is a relatively modern term for a centuries-old technique. It was practised by the Greeks and Romans and developed by Renaissance and Baroque artists. The Romans delighted in illusions painted by artists on their villa walls. Scenes of landscapes, gardens, and architectural fantasies visually enlarged the space in the rooms. Around A.D. 300, the Roman writer Philostratus the Younger wrote that deception in art is pleasurable: "… to confront objects which do not exist as though they existed, and to be influenced by them, to believe that they do exist, is not this, since no harm can come of it, a suitable and irreproachable means of providing entertainment?"

After the fall of Rome, attempts at illusion and trompe l'œil were rare. However, in the Romanesque baptisteries of the chapels of the kings of Majorca at Perpignan in France and Majorca in Spain there are wall paintings simulating arches and pillars. These are considered remarkable because perspective is lacking in paintings of the eleventh and twelfth century.

From Roman times, however, various systems and devices were used to suggest distance and represent space in paintings, but not until the Renaissance was a method of measurement devised for creating perspective. Once artists had mastered the principles of linear perspective, murals developed into true three-dimensional illusions of space.

previous page:
This painting of doors within doors adds a visual extension to a hallway. If a trompe l'œil mural like this is to deceive the viewer, the artist must achieve a convincing three-dimensional effect by means of perspective drawing and the use of colour, shading, shadows, and contrast.
MURALISTS: ROBERTA GORDON-SMITH

◀ **A mural has transformed** the flat walls surrounding a London swimming pool with a scene across sculpted gardens to a distant, wooded landscape. In this view-through-the-wall, the swimmer's eye is caught by the exotic colours of peacocks, and led outward to graceful statues, carved balustrades, formal parterres, and past the conical outlines of cypresses to a false horizon. The portico that frames this view gives the mural a classical air.
MURALIST: JANET SHEARER

In the early 1400s the Florentine architects Filipo Brunelleschi (1377–1446) and Leon Battista Alberti (1404–72) discovered and developed linear perspective. This is essentially a system that enables artists to measure the apparent changes in scale of objects as they recede into the distance – or into the background of a painting – and so represent them as the eye sees them.

This discovery was a revelation in the study of art and architecture, for although various devices had been used in the past to suggest distance in drawings and paintings, no one, until then, had succeeded in devising a way of applying measurements to a scene in order to reproduce it realistically. Brunelleschi based his perspective system on the simple observation that receding parallel lines appear to meet in the distance or at the horizon at the viewer's eye level. The point where the lines seem to converge – the vanishing point – can be calculated mathematically and plotted on a wall or a canvas.

Linear perspective was explored by its discoverers and their contemporaries. The Florentine artist, Masaccio (1401–c. 1428) appears to have been the first notable artist to apply it to painting: in his fresco in the Church of Santa Maria Novella in Florence, Italy, *The Holy Trinity, with the Virgin, St. John and Donors*, he painted figures to a realistic scale; set them in a unified space; made a tomb appear to project into a church, and painted a chapel as if it were seen through a wall. Perspective, used with contrasts of light and shade and changing colour tone, enabled artists to give a new dimension to the space represented in their paintings. An image could now be painted as if it had broken through the wall surface into the space beyond.

previous page:
Informal parkland was the theme chosen for a mural painted in oils to surround this beautiful swimming pool in an urban pied à terre. The neoclassical columns are real, while the "stone" balustrade is painted. In this detail, the curved pool edge is mirrored in the rounded shape of the lake in the mural. No people, no animals, disturb this quiet scene, but there is movement: paintbrushes and other objects suggest a presence recently departed; and, lifted by a ruffle of breeze, a page of music flutters from its stand.
MURALIST: IAN CAIRNIE

▶ **The muralist** has captured an atmosphere of stillness in this garden enclosure, painted in oils on the wall of a city dining room. The illusion that the view beyond the real dining room wall recedes to a walled garden is highlighted by the contrast between the miniature orange trees in tubs on the stone balustrade, and the tidy, well-kept garden behind them. The owner, a keen gardener, is just about to pick up the garden fork set down on the wall – and the bird that has just escaped from the open cage is perched on an urn in a mural on the dining room's opposite wall.
MURALIST: JONATHAN BRUNSKILL

The artists of the Italian Renaissance who developed perspective techniques and the illusionistic devices of trompe l'œil achieved extraordinarily high technical and esthetic standards in wall painting. They perfected fresco, a physically demanding technique in which paint is applied directly onto the final layer of wet plaster. They had to complete each section of the work before the plaster dried, and so could paint only a small area of wall at a time.

Modern muralists rarely use fresco because it can be so time-consuming. They work instead in acrylics and oils, which are more practical. Frescoes are also permanent, and because people these days tend to live in one place for only a short time, many murals are painted on canvas before being positioned on a wall, so that they can easily be moved.

Murals painted in acrylics or oils are more pollution-resistant than frescoes. Many ancient wall-paintings have only been preserved because their location in caves or in tombs has protected them from the damp atmosphere, or because natural disturbances, such as volcanic eruptions, have buried them. Medieval murals painted in northern Europe have not survived so well as those in the warmer, drier Mediterranean climate. However, in a ruined church in the county of Norfolk, England, two ancient frescoes have recently been found, concealed beneath ivy and two plaster layers. The oldest has been dated to the 1200s and the other to the 1600s. These Romanesque paintings may be the oldest extensive church frescoes in Britain.

▲ **Ruined Gothic cloisters** frame a hazy vista across an Italianate landscape in this mural, entitled *Shelley in Italy*. The painting creates an illusion of space and depth and even seems to illuminate the hallway it decorates. A lizard basks in the sunlight, patiently waiting to be noticed. Such delightful trompe l'œil details which artists add to their paintings may go unnoticed at first; but once discovered, they enchant the beholder and complement the magical sense of illusion. The muralist's keen interest in watercolour is seen in the light style of this mural.
MURALIST: SOPHIA BARRATT

Blurring the boundary between living space and landscape, house and garden, has been an important role for murals for a millennium or more. Using techniques such as linear perspective, the correct mathematical relationship between the sizes of objects close up and in the distance, and the perceived changes in hue and tone that occur as objects recede, an artist can effect an illusion of distance and space in a painting and so recreate a landscape on the walls of a room.

Painted vistas of landscapes or gardens, inspired by the plantings surrounding their country villas and the views from their terraces, were a favourite interior design theme for Romans living in the first century B.C., a period known as the Second Style of Pompeian Painting. In his book on architecture written for Augustus Caesar, the Roman military architect Vitruvius described the fashion of his younger days for walls "decorated with landscapes of various sorts, modelling these images on the features of actual places. In these are painted harbours, promontories, coastlines, rivers, springs, sanctuaries, groves, mountains, flocks, and shepherds". It seems from archeological records that Romans preferred decorating their walls to filling their houses with furniture. Their murals were planned according to a room's layout, so that visitors would be impressed from some distance away.

Livia, the wife of Augustus Caesar, was the owner of a villa in which the mural of a garden, reproduced opposite, was originally painted for the main wall of the garden room. Elements of nature were used to create this lovely scene, with trees fading gently into the distance.

Writing in his old age, Vitruvius lamented the passing of this phase of naturalism in murals. In his book he criticized the then modern tastes for other themes in wall painting and sadly reflected on fashions for landscapes in bygone eras. These "representations derived from reality" he complained to Augustus Caesar in his book, "are now scorned by the undiscriminating tastes of the present". But the fashion returned, repeatedly, throughout history. Rediscovered Roman wall paintings inspired landscape murals during the neoclassical period – the late 1700s and early 1800s – and have continued to do so into modern times. The painting of Livia's villa garden is as appealing today as it must have been for the empress for whom it was painted. Its simplicity and easy style mean that it is not too difficult to recreate and its delightful freshness has inspired copies on contemporary walls.

While creating deep perspective in murals requires artistic skill, aerial perspective is easier to effect. The suggestion of depth is achieved, for instance, by painting objects close to the observer in more detail than those in the distance. Against a muted background of blue-grey hills, a floral border is framed, perhaps, by dark hedges and backed by tall hollyhocks, lupins, foxgloves, daisies, irises, tulips, and other summer blooms provide splashes of primary colour reminiscent of a painting by the French artist Claude Monet (1840–1926). And meadows of bright green grasses scattered with lacy cow parsley, fritillaries, buttercups, daisies, and poppies, might fade into the misty pale gray tones of a distant horizon.

◄ **This Roman garden scene** was originally painted on the wall of the garden room in a country house called Villa Livia in Prima Porta outside Rome, owned by Livia, wife of the great Roman emperor, Augustus Caesar. A narrow area in the foreground is separated from the rest of the garden by a low fence, a visual device which encourages a sense of recession. From the detail of a citrus orange tree in fruit it can be seen that more attention has been given to the trees and birds in the foreground, while the background fades into the muted tones of the distance.
LOCATION: MUSEO NAZIONALE ROMANO, ROME

◄ **Livia's garden** (above) clearly inspired this modern interpretation. The flower, bird, butterfly, and other foreground details are crisp, capturing the freshness of a real garden, but they melt into the background, which gives the landscape a tranquil feeling. The mural is painted in acrylics directly onto plaster and extends across 2 feet (6.5 metres) of three low walls of a modern orangery filled with natural light.
MURALIST: CAROLINE COWLEY

▲ ▶ **A feast of images** covers all four walls of this large dining room. The mural appears to look out from inside a marquee onto a formal garden. The artist's client had just moved house and wanted reminders of life in the family's former home to be painted in the mural. This dream garden, where a red cardinal sings and a monkey brandishes a bottle, depicts parkland near the owner's last home. The monumental column on the right, mirrored by tall parkland trees, is a detail from another part of the mural. It is beautifully painted to look like the mighty support of some ancient ruined temple, and it gives the garden a neoclassical feel. Transfixed by its majestic scale, the viewer may fail, at first, to spot the leopard crouched on a bough of a stately tree in the middle distance. This striking detail has special meaning for the owner.
MURALIST: IAN CAIRNIE

Comparatively few people commission easel paintings, although they may occasionally buy paintings from a gallery, but increasing numbers of people are commissioning murals. Most murals are, therefore, original works of art. Few are faithful copies of wall paintings that survive from the past, and those which are inspired by the work of other artists always carry the muralist's "signature" in terms of personal style and original features.

A mural can be an exclusively personal form of interior decoration, as well as an original one. The concept may originate with the client, and, while working out a scheme with the muralist, he or she may request the inclusion of some object, detail, or even person in the painting that is especially meaningful. Such personal details make every mural exclusive.

A muralist is both a decorative artist and an actor waiting to be offered a role in which to ingeniously interpret the clients' wishes. This is the view of Ian Cairnie, a muralist of 25 years' standing, whose client list is world-wide. Scenes from his design for a dining room are illustrated opposite. The mural covers all four walls, including a swing door through to the kitchen, which is disguised behind the painted wrought iron gate on the left. Real wall lamps have been subtly integrated into the painting, being apparently attached to painted tent poles. The painted foliage and balustrades on the left cover low built-in cupboards, which open at a light touch. Thus, the artist has blended all of the functional elements and fittings on the wall into his ravishing scenery.

When a mural is to be seen from a comparatively close proximity – as is this one by diners seated around the table – Cairnie believes that the picture should unfold before the viewers' eyes as they take in more and more of the panorama and gradually notice the details. In this fascinating, detailed work it is hard to know where to rest the eye. So much is to be seen in this view "through the walls" of the dining room out to distant landscapes with their varieties of trees, streams, an ornate bridge, sculptural urns, water spouting from a drinking fountain, ivy spreading down the damp, stained stonework to which it clings, and countless other images. Among them are many details requested by the client. One is a monkey, mischievously tantalizing diners with a bottle of wine; another is a leopard in a tree, a personal reminder of a story attached to the parkland depicted in the mural.

Parks, gardens, and landscapes are themes especially suited to an apartment or house in a city, where space is at a premium and beautiful rural views are in short supply. The peaceful atmosphere of an illusion of nature painted on a wall makes it an appropriate subject for lobbies, stairwells, living rooms, kitchens, and windowless basements.

There are places, however, where a landscape seems singularly inappropriate and a muralist may find it impossible to gratify a client's wishes. Such was the case when a business client wished to commission Cairnie to paint the concrete walls of his nuclear shelter in Switzerland with a trompe l'œil landscape. This unlikely prospect was made more daunting for the artist by the need to paint the mural on site, directly onto the wall.

An illusion of a garden is a great way to realize a fantasy of a dream land-scape, whether its elements and features are indigenous to one's own country or are the rural idyll of another. The captivating landscapes photographed for postcards sent by friends on holiday abroad, or collected on our own travels, are often eventually relegated to the backs of drawers after having been pinned for months on notice boards in kitchens. These often superb photographic images seem too beautiful to throw away and may have a sentimental value associated with their location. Instead of reluctantly discarding these mementoes when the day comes for the annual rejection of clutter, why not use them as inspiration for a mural depicting a place with strong personal memories?

For details, gardening magazines are useful sources of ideas for walls, gates, trees, hedges, and garden ornaments such as urns, ponds, and fountains, as well as plants and flowers native to different parts of the world. And interior design magazines are illustrated with photographs of landscapes and garden styles, terraces, courtyards, and planting schemes.

▶ **A formal garden** with distant views decorates the wall of this dining room. A trellis prettily planted with trailing roses conceals an off-centre door in an angled wall. The trellis, painted up the door, arching over it, and continuing down the wall to the right, restores the visual balance and draws the eye to the urn at its centre. The artist has depicted her clients as statues behind the parterre, painted their country house in the landscape, and included their favourite flowers and birds in the mural. The sky is light and airy to maximize the height of the low-ceilinged room.
MURALIST: HELEN BARNES

◀ **A Parisian square** seen from a verandah is the subject of this recent mural by an English artist living in Paris. The painted wooden framework of a conservatory provides a structure that links the room with the view through imaginary glazed windows into the courtyard beyond. The mural decorates the wall of a salon on the ground floor of a hotel in central Paris and depicts the view from the hotel terrace.
MURALIST: MARIE BYNG

As long as there have been gardens, artists have painted them as decorations for walls and artefacts. Before the Romans painted them on their villa walls, Persian carpet makers wove ornamental gardens into rugs and wall hangings, and Egyptian painters depicted them on tomb walls.

Formal gardens with their decorative arbours, arches, pools, statuary, and colourful flower beds surrounding paved courts or green swards make charming wall paintings. Straight paths, fences, and the edges of lawns and planted beds are tools an artist can use to create perspective effects. And window frames, shutters, balustrades, and low fences are all trompe l'œil devices that can be utilized in the foreground to aid the transition from interior space to the created vista and heighten the illusion of distance.

Garden structures may also be used by a clever muralist to overcome problems posed by walls with awkward angles and permanent fixtures, such as doors and cupboards. To the English muralist Helen Barnes, designing a mural to camouflage such unesthetic features is an enjoyable challenge. In one of her murals, illustrated opposite, colourful blooms are painted in the foreground, a device that has long been used to enhance perspective where an indication of depth is needed, both in paintings and in real gardens. Gertrude Jekyll (1843–1932), an English garden designer, planted polychromatic borders to indicate perspective in garden design. She used gradations of colour with the eye of a painter: sharp, brightly coloured blooms in the foreground receding to taller flowers in blues and grays at the back.

The painting of a garden square in central Paris, illustrated above, continues a tradition established by the Impressionist artists and their associates. Edouard Manet (1832–83), Claude Monet (1840–1926), and Auguste Renoir (1841–1919) loved to paint the Parisian Parc Monceau, with its extraordinary juxtapositions of colourful flowers. Later, Monet established, planted, and repeatedly painted his famous garden at Giverny near Rouen.

► **This mural recreates** the lost view from a window that was converted into a door. The window looked out onto this garden with a planted trellis in the foreground and a dense growth of garden trees visible behind it. Two butterflies – one shown in detail on the right – endow the mural with the atmosphere of a summer's day, and so invest the room with a feeling of warmth all year long.
MURALIST: RICHARD BAGGULEY

In a prestigious London apartment muralist Richard Bagguley painted the trompe l'œil illustrated above to recreate a lost view. The interior designer had the problem of restoring the balance of a room space that had been altered by the removal of a window. Originally, two windows were positioned side by side in the kitchen, through which a garden could be seen. But part of the kitchen was extended to form a new dining room and one window had to be converted into a door, destroying the symmetry. Bagguley's solution was to paint a trompe l'œil on the new door so that it looked like the window it had replaced, and recreate the view from the original window – of a plant-entwined trellis. Solving interior design anomalies such as this is fascinating for an inventive muralist who can draw on experience and ingenuity to find decorative solutions.

Artists often find it convenient to paint a mural on canvas and later attach it to the wall at the chosen site. Sometimes, however, they may choose to paint directly onto a wall or door on-site. The apartment in which Richard Bagguley's mural was to be painted was unoccupied, and painting the scene in situ was an advantage: to see what he was painting, all the muralist had to do was pop his head round the corner and study the view.

Murals of gardens have been commissioned to adorn not only the immovable walls of brick buildings but the less-solid room divisions of a more transient location: a ship's cabin. The detail above is part of a mural in the Conservatory Restaurant aboard the P&O cruise liner *Oriana*.

Following in the footsteps of John Piper, who painted murals for an earlier cruise ship *Oriana*, the English muralist Colin Failes was commissioned to paint a mural across seven panels to run along the restaurant wall of a new cruise ship. Failes researched his theme for an English garden at the Royal Horticultural Society's Headquarters at Wisley, outside London, where there is a library and many acres of gardens displaying plants of every type. The mural contains some 50 different plant species and varieties.

A patio area that appears to extend outward from just behind the diners' seating gives an impression of space that could be stepped into before continuing along the pathway to the garden's horizon. This may be an intentional diversion from the vista of the ocean that diners can see through the dining room's plate glass windows. The greens of lawns, foliage and trees predominate in this painting, and green, the spectrum's central hue, is a calming colour, easy on the eye.

▲ **A ship's dining room** is decorated with this garden scene of a terrace bordered with raised beds, and steps rising to a wide green lawn. Through the garden's boundary wall there are glimpses of a distant horizon. Continuity is given to the panels by two large terracotta pots symmetrically placed on the wall, brimming with bright blooms.
MURALIST: COLIN FAILES

◄ **False swagged curtains** frame the windows and seem to fill a corner of a dining room. This mural was painted in the Quinta de São Sebastião, an old farmhouse in Portugal built around 1780, and the name of the artist is long forgotten. The mural has the effect of harmonizing the sharply angled corner with painted details on the walls and ceilings of the surrounding rooms.

▶ A trompe l'œil door panel
shows doors opening onto a
balcony, where a table is laid for
breakfast. This painting depicts
a view within a view, for from
the balcony there is a vista over
a swimming pool and beyond it
to a forest. The panel, in acrylics
on canvas and 6 feet 3 inches
(1.8 metres) high, was painted
for a 1984 exhibition at Trompe
L'Oeil Gallery, New York.
MURALIST: LINCOLN SELIGMAN

◀ **Rus in urbe** – traditional, white-painted houses, tall cypress trees and an azure sky lend a new dimension to the wall of a Parisian apartment. The staircase becomes part of the mural, which creates an illusion of height and extended space beyond the wall. Shadows cast by the trees suggest permanent sunlight and the inviting terrace has promises of vistas across the misty shores of the Aegean or the Mediterranean.
MURALISTS: DOMINIQUE MARAVAL, FABIENNE ARIETTI

▶ **The horizon** in these two panels at the top of a stairwell is painted in line with the real horizon, which can be glimpsed through the window on the left. This provides a visual link between the painted landscape and the real one. To increase the illusion of depth, trompe l'œils of large vases of flowers have been painted on what appear to be window sills.
MURALIST: COLIN FAILES

Walls above staircases are often uninteresting areas, usually sparsely decorated with framed paintings, prints, or photographs. But a picture can be lost in these narrow areas of wall. A mural in such a situation can provide a stylish decorative element, but also a useful illusionary one.

The two panels illustrated are from a three-panel mural painted on a stairway descending to an indoor swimming pool. The arched painted windows at the top of the stairwell break the monotony of an imposing tall and narrow wall, and reflect a view of the gentle countryside around the house. The mural illustrated on the left can be seen from the living area in the foreground of the photograph. The mural covers the entire wall area, successfully enlivening the otherwise featureless staircase, which the muralist has cleverly integrated into the mural.

Architectural fantasies have been used to decorate walls for centuries. Trompe l'œil, being decorative and relatively inexpensive, was used instead of stonework and carving by Roman and Renaissance artists. It is more versatile, able to simulate effects that cannot be achieved in real architecture. A building within a building was the effect created in some Roman murals, which depict columns in the foreground of a view of an architectural perspective. Renaissance artists excelled in illusions of architecture in interiors. One important example – not illustrated here – is a fresco of about 1516 by Renaissance architect and painter Baldassare Peruzzi (1481–1536) showing a simulated view of Rome through trompe l'œil columns, which look convincingly like part of the room's real architecture.

From the early 1600s the art of illusionistic painting underwent a magnificent flowering. It became an essential component in the buildings of the Roman sculptor-architects, Gianlorenzo Bernini (1598–1680) and Francesco Borromini (1599–1667). Rejecting the artistic and architectural ideals of the Renaissance, they designed buildings based on geometric forms, mainly curves (the style that evolved from their work was later called Baroque, thought to be derived from a Portuguese word meaning "misshapen"). They fused architecture, sculpture, and painting in their buildings, especially their churches, many of which were conceived on a vast scale, and often dramatically lit inside to give a flickering impression of movement. An integral part of Baroque buildings were walls and vaults richly adorned with illusionistic paintings and false architectural perspectives. The Palazzo Spada in Rome has a famous trompe l'œil gallery by Borromini (not illustrated here), which gives the impression of vast length, but is only a few feet long.

▼ **A view from** one building is transported to another in this mural in the entrance lobby of the Philip Morris Company building in Rockefeller Center. The muralist has effected an extension of visual space that takes the eye not just outward by a breathtaking distance but also up to the apparently vertiginous height of the imaginary rooftop.
MURALIST: RICHARD HAAS

► **A sofa rests** against a wall of *faux* relief carving beside steps leading to a building, perhaps Roman or Romanesque in style. A mysterious Gothic edifice – castle or cathedral – looms out of the dawn landscape behind. This medley of architectural style and symbolism overlooks a family room in a villa in Cortona in Tuscany, northern Italy.

▼ **This window on ancient Athens** was commissioned by a restaurateur from Cyprus, the owner of the Burger King chain, for a new branch in northern England. In the centre panel is the Acropolis, restored to its pristine appearance; the right-hand panel shows the exterior of a theatre, painstakingly restored by the artist. The mural was painted in panels to fit between real columns – and the muralist had to work into the scheme the uplighting washing the walls. This mural on the ground floor is mirrored by another on the floor above, showing the same view from a higher perspective.
MURALISTS: DAVIES, KEELING, TROWBRIDGE

The old idea of apparently breaking through a wall by projecting a painted scene or view through a false opening in it is particularly useful for enlivening a long wall with no interesting features. The American artist, Richard Haas, painted the mural opposite to transform the north wall of Nelson Atrium, a loft in a 1976 building on Canal Street in New York City. In this mural he also made superb use of the visual devices of trompe l'œil, including perspective, detail, light, and shade, to extend the room visually. The wall of the loft disappears and is replaced with a scene of Renaissance architecture. The eye is drawn through archways supported on colonnades, across courtyards to a distant square flanked by elegant buildings.

Haas began his career studying fine art at the University of Wisconsin, Milwaukee. The architectural emphasis of his paintings may perhaps be explained by influences in his youth, when he assisted his great uncle, a stonemason employed by the great American architect, Frank Lloyd Wright (1869-1959). Wright placed strong emphasis on the integration of building and environment. Haas painted his first view-through-a-wall in his loft/studio on Greene Street, New York (illustrated on page 118), in 1974. He has since transformed walls all over the U.S.A. with magnificent architectural illusions.

Although he has painted architectural fantasies in many interiors, Haas is better known for his monumental murals on exterior walls. A spectacular example – not shown here – is his conversion of the side elevation of the Brotherhood Building, headquarters of the Kroger Company of Cincinnati, into a fantasy view of a grandiose Roman temple. This dramatic mural, inspired by a reconstruction of the ancient Roman Temple of Vesta by the Baroque artist Giovanni Battista Piranesi (c. 1720–28), seems so real that the curving staircase appears to project into the company's parking lot at the foot of the building.

Simulating the rich architecture of the past is the speciality of this artist. His admiration for historical architecture and dislike of the insensitivity of modern urban planning are messages unmistakably conveyed by the trans-formations Haas wreaks on the often bleak façades of twentieth-century buildings. Unremarkable edifices in many American cities have been dramatically altered by his illusionistic skills, and as a result he is now widely recognized internationally as a master of trompe l'œil, and credited with having rediscov-ered the genre in modern times.

Haas first shocked the American establishment in the mid-1970s, when he proposed to paint the shadows of architectural masterpieces on the side elevations of less esthetically pleasing buildings. He planned, for example, to decorate the north sides of the World Trade Center towers in New York with shadows of the Empire State and the Chrysler Buildings. His criticism of urban planning decisions implicit in this proposal caused outrage, especially since he suggested painting the silhouettes of buildings that have been destroyed, such as Stanford White's Madison Square Garden in New York, on the sides of inferior buildings near where they once stood. His expressed intention in these proposals was to pay tribute to architects of the past.

Haas later developed this idea by evoking in his murals haunting memories of demolished landmarks. One example is his mural on the Centre Theatre, Milwaukee, Wisconsin. On the side wall he painted mirror-glass which seems to reflect the view of the city – including the old Pabst Building, a tower erected around 1910 which once stood nearby. Haas was raised in Wisconsin and knew the building well. It was still standing when he was commissioned to paint the mural and was torn down while his was at the planning stage. He modified his design to include the Pabst Building in his imaginary reflection of the city, and painted it complete with its pinnacle, which had been removed in the 1950s.

"Walls present some of the most interesting and challenging surfaces in an urban area" Haas told a reporter from *Time* magazine in a recent interview. "I look at them as large canvases for an artist to come and paint on."

▶ **A functional interior wall** is transmuted by a trompe l'œil, which appears to invite the viewer to step through it, back in time to Renaissance Rome. The colonnaded archway directs the gaze out to the distant courtyard of the Palazzo Farnese in Rome. This was the masterpiece of the leading High Renaissance architect, Antonio da Sangallo the younger (1485–1546), which was completed after his death by Michelangelo. An illusory light casts shadows across the floor of this apparent extension of the room, and the courtyard beyond is bathed in sunlight. Nelson Atrium in New York City, where this mural was painted, was demolished in 1987, but the mural was removed and is now in storage.
MURALIST: RICHARD HAAS

▲ **This detail** is part of a mural scheme for the Smithsonian Institution's underground Quadrangle Museum complex in Washington D.C. The detail shows the lower wall, on which the muralist has painted a perspective view through the ruins of a classical building to one of the original Victorian museum buildings.
MURALIST: RICHARD HAAS

Richard Haas is credited with having advanced the frontiers of trompe l'œil in some of his most ambitious works, which combine fantasy with illusion, an element of realism, and biting social comment. His mural of the Fontainebleau Hotel in Miami Beach, Florida, is an outstanding example. The view from the ocean front and the highway of this popular building by Morris Lapidus, an architect whose work was popular during the 1950s, was insensitively obscured by the blank back wall of a seven-storey building. Haas responded by painting on the blank wall a perfect replica of the lost view, framed by a triumphal arch in Art Deco style, and flanked by two huge caryatids.

Although paintings on building exteriors are outside the scope of this book, they can and do influence interior decoration. As well as transforming bland, characterless towers and blocks, architectural murals can be painted indoors to remind people of more elegant and romantic buildings that may once have existed in their cities. Community and spontaneous street art is appearing in urban areas everywhere. Even the hoardings erected to cover

unsightly building work are now often covered by murals – which sometimes reflect an image of the planned new architecture. These developments demonstrate that people need to mask the harsh reality of a concrete and brick environment with bright, lively images.

A sympathy for the art and architecture of the past is shared by many muralists. Catherine Lovegrove, a respected English artist who has painted murals in Asia and Africa, the U.K. and Europe, and the U.S.A., is one. Lovegrove collects inspiration from many, varied sources of painting and architecture, and although she has painted murals on a wide variety of themes, and may be influenced by one of her favourite artists, or a painter particularly admired by one of her clients, her own distinct painting style prevails. She is sometimes assisted on her projects by other artists.

This mural was painted directly onto cupboard units, but for wall paintings Lovegrove uses a technique called marouflage. She paints the mural on canvas in her studio and applies the canvas directly onto the wall at the site.

▲ **Architecture in Palladian style** frames a sea view, influenced by the French painter of the 1600s, Claude Lorrain, in this mural painted across the front of fitted cupboard units that cover a whole wall. To make the view convincing when it is seen from different angles in the room, the muralist has utilized a system of three-point perspective (that is, using three vanishing points).
MURALIST: CATHERINE LOVEGROVE

◄ **A view across the waters of an eastern sea** is the theme of this mural, one of a series of three painted on the walls of a large private dining room, on which are scattered the white triangular lateen sails of wooden dhows – traditional Arab sailing vessels. In the foreground is a dish of oranges – once an exotic oriental fruit on European tables. Each painting, in acrylics, is 8 feet high by 3 feet wide (2.4 metres by 0.9 metres). When the series was completed, the paintings were installed in the client's home in arched alcoves surrounded by simulated stone walls. Real red velvet curtains were then draped on either side to enhance the impression of a Middle Eastern interior, created by the room's tented ceiling.
MURALIST: STEPHEN ROBERTS

Using perspective effects a muralist can make a wall metamorphose into a panoramic view across the sea. Majestic coastal scenery and the romantic shores of oceanic islands are perhaps less common subjects for murals than rural landscapes, but there are notable examples painted both by famous muralists of the past, such as the English artist Rex Whistler (1905–44), and by respected contemporary muralists.

The paintings illustrated on these pages, by the British muralist Stephen Roberts, depict an imaginary view north across the Mediterranean Sea from the North African coast. The artist has captured in his superb use of colour the intense heat of a North African summer: the white stone of the buildings suggests strong sunlight, and the azure sea mirrors the blue of the cloudless sky, which recedes to a misty whitish haze toward the horizon.

The sea and sky are framed in these murals by buildings recalling the architecture of the Islamic Empire, with horseshoe arches, lattice windows, pierced and tiled walls, and scalloped decoration. Traditional building style often plays a major part in evoking the romantic atmosphere of a sea view. A sharp horizon placed low in a view of a deep blue sea, seen through a gap between flat-roofed, whitewashed houses, might suggest, for example, an elevated outlook from a hilly Aegean or Mediterranean island.

Stephen Roberts's flair for decorative detail is apparent from the objects in these murals. His decorative and trompe l'œil work – mainly small, intimate paintings – have appeared in many London shows over two decades.

▲ **Traditional artefacts from the souks** – colourful carpets, metal pots, ceramic jars decorated with geometric designs – give this mural, the second in a series of three, an authentic North African feel. Details such as the beautiful inlaid table (above) are a speciality of the versatile muralist, whose decorative work ranges from textile design to designs for objets d'art.
MURALIST: STEPHEN ROBERTS

A sea mural is an appropriate subject for a wall anywhere, even in a dim or windowless room, where careful illumination with warm lighting can simulate sunlight. A view with a clear, wide horizon is appropriate as a decoration for a room with a long wall, such as an extension, and for a space lit from above by a glass roof or a skylight. Sea views are also ideal subjects for walls with good natural illumination.

Trompe l'œil murals of sea views are often commissioned for public buildings, especially for restaurants. A logical, but somehow unexpected location for a mural of the sea is on a ship, yet more than one cruise liner has a mural on a sea theme.

▲ **This unusual sea view,** entitled *Dream World*, overlooks the dining room of a ship of Norwegian Cruise Lines, SS *Dreamward*, which sails the seas around Florida. The American muralist has painted an imaginary underwater scene, a romantic view of a coral reef – of which there are many in the shallow waters around the Caribbean islands – and reef fish of the region, with divers exploring a wreck.
MURALIST: RICHARD HAAS

The range of moods that may be induced by a sea view mural seems unending, ranging from waves breaking on coral sands fringed with palms to more dramatic northern coastal scenes with the still waters of inlets and lochs reflecting high headlands. Most people associate the sea with holiday locations full of pleasurable memories and a tropical haven on a wall can be an instant escape route from a stressful lifestyle or an uninspiring climate.

Escapism is the explicit theme of the murals illustrated opposite. The long, low wall surrounding a very modern swimming pool room with a glass roof in a private house in the county of Surrey, southern England, is completely covered by the seascape (top), supposedly surrounding the pool and the house. It depicts a dreamily hazy distant Caribbean island in a turquoise tropical sea framed by tall columns painted in the style of a classical temple. The colour of the sea echoes the colour of the water in the swimming pool. During the cold months between autumn and spring the mural imbues the room with the atmosphere of a hot summer in the tropics. During the English summer months it is removed and stored so that real french windows running the length of the room behind it can be opened to reveal the view of the garden outside.

A panoramic vista has to look real to someone seeing it from any angle, or walking past it from extreme right to extreme left. To achieve this, an artist may need to employ systems of perspective, often calculating many vanish-

▶ **This mural of a tropical seascape** off the Barbados coast gives the impression that swimmers can climb out of the swimming pool and walk across the deck and down the stairs to a sandy beach. The mural is 40 feet (36.6 metres) long and painted on 16 panels, each 2 feet 6 inches (7.6 metres) wide – 10 panels are visible in this illustration. The panels are hung in a 'curtain wall' arrangement, so that they can be taken down for storage in summer. The artist used acrylics and finished the mural with acrylic matt varnish for protection from humidity.
MURALIST: COLIN FAILES

◀ **An exotic view** across a golden beach on one of Thailand's beautiful offshore islands is the subject of this mural for a Thai restaurant in London. Traditional Thai fishing boats moored at the beachside contribute to the mural's oriental atmosphere, and the shape of the great limestone rock projecting from the sea recalls the sail of a fishing junk.
MURALIST: DAVIES, KEELING, TROWBRIDGE

ing points (points at which receding parallel lines appear to meet in the distance). In a seascape, placing the horizon line low can create a dramatic sense of space and distance. Including a prominent object in the foreground enhances the illusion of depth – by appearing to push the view further into the background of the picture, and by providing a contrast with the size of features far away.

The mural above is an exotic view from a beach resort in the Far East. The distinctive landscape of southern Thailand is an important feature of this painting. Tables set for dinner in the foreground suggest a romantic evening on a beach terrace beneath a tropical night sky. Jutting out in the middle distance is a limestone monolith, a feature of the southern Thai shores.

◀ **Rich turquoise shades** carry the eye to the clear line of the distant horizon. This ocean view seems to open the wall and create a sense of space in the room. The painting of the sea is viewed through a trompe l'œil window frame in the same style as the panelled mirror and real window frame – a clever device through which the mural is integrated with the room's architecture. The realism of the scene, confirmed by binoculars hanging tantalizingly from the painted window frame, their weight and form perfectly rendered, seems tangible – the waves can almost be heard.

From ancient times to the present, a universal fascination with birds and animals, added to their diverse forms and beautiful coloration, have made them perennially favourite subjects for murals. They are an essential component of landscape scenes, make ornamental features in garden murals, and appear as decorative details in murals of almost every genre, adding a splash of colour here, a surprise element there. In trompe l'œil murals their role is often to make the illusion the artist presents as reality seem more convincing.

Birds and animals feature large among the plants, shells, and other natural subjects which are the favourite themes of Graham Rust, the celebrated British muralist. His trompe l'œil wall and ceiling paintings are in many houses and churches in Europe and the U.S.A.

Rust's greatest work is perhaps his series of murals and ceiling paintings in Ragley Hall in the county of Warwickshire in central England, the historic seat of the Marquess and Marchioness of Hertford. The spectacular decoration of the staircase walls and ceiling took him more than ten years to complete. The main theme of this work is the Temptation of Christ as described in the New Testament. It was the choice of Lord Hertford, who had visited the Mount of Temptation in Israel. The Devil tempting Christ is the subject of the central ceiling decoration; and around the walls of the vast stairwell the artist has painted the kingdoms of the world – the riches which Christ denied. The mural is full of images relating to the family. A peacock, for instance, standing on a stone urn covered in relief sculptures, represents the many beautiful birds belonging to their estate.

In his early twenties, Rust visited the Villa Maser near Treviso in northeast Italy and was impressed and inspired by the vibrant illusionistic frescos of the Renaissance artist Paolo Veronese (c. 1528–1588), which fill every room. Now an artist whose own work inspires others, Rust has published two books of sketches and drawings, with photographs of his finished works and helpful information on the planning of murals.

▶ **Country life in the 1600s** is the overall theme of the mural from which this is a detail. The painting was commissioned for the owners of a country house which was designed in the Palladian manner by Quinlan Terry, a noted twentieth-century British neoclassical architect, who expressed a wish that the hall and stairwell be painted. Pheasants – the birds most closely associated with life in the great houses of rural England – stand on an ornamental stone urn against a background of the parkland surrounding the house.
MURALIST: GRAHAM RUST

◀ **The bright hues of animals and plants** stand out among the muted tones of sculptural and architectural detail and the subdued shades of this mural's background landscape. This detail is from the ground floor section of the mural at Ragley Hall in the British Midlands. On the lower walls the artist has painted toucans and a roseate spoonbill from South America, and two African monkeys in perfect detail, their shapes and colours harmonizing with the neutral shades of columns and follies in the background. Elsewhere a cheetah sits on an ornamental urn, chained by a broad red collar to a column.
MURALIST: GRAHAM RUST

▲ **This delightful monkey** is one of many highly detailed studies of natural subjects by this notable British muralist. It appears as a detail in the mural on the right, costumed in the manner of the 1600s, in accord with the period decoration of the house.
MURALIST: GRAHAM RUST

◄ **A resplendent peacock** perches on an unprepossessing radiator housing. The shape of its folded tail feathers is mirrored by a cascade of real flowers in a vase purposely positioned beside it. This unexpected, provocative vision instantly attracts the visitor's interest and holds it, diverting all attention away from the fixture beneath it.
MURALIST: CAROLINE COWLEY

◄ **Three guinea fowl** cling, improbably, to an architrave. This trompe l'œil trick, made for no reason other than to indulge a sense of artistic fun, cannot fail to startle newcomers; and the beautifully painted birds will continue to be decorative long after they have ceased to deceive their owner's eye.
MURALIST: JANET SHEARER

Peacocks with their iridescent feathers and regal air are an irresistible challenge for muralists. These supremely beautiful birds, native to tropical forests on the Indian subcontinent, were common in Roman and Persian art, and they have been staple subject matter for muralists for centuries. They have most commonly provided the decorative and colourful foreground focus in landscape murals, but they are sometimes made the main subject of a mural. Many other exotic birds – parrots, cockatoos, birds of paradise, ibises, flamingos, cardinals – can make wonderfully decorative additions to modern murals. Individual muralists will sometimes favour certain birds, such as swans or pheasants. For example, the English muralist Graham Rust has a special admiration for spoonbills (see page 88).

Birds with brightly coloured plumage are often judiciously positioned to attract the viewer's eye to a particular area of a mural. They are also apt subjects for odd, isolated locations in a room. Muralists find them ideal material for brightening gloomy corners and for distracting the eye from unattractive features and ugly fixtures, such as water pipes and radiators. And they will sometimes paint a bird in the most unexpected location for the sheer pleasure of its unjustifiable presence. The guinea fowl in the photograph above would scarcely be seen perched on an architrave in real life – but fantasy is often the essence of a mural, and this gives the artist an excuse to create a unique decorative feature just for fun.

This element of surprise can enhance the deceptive effect of a small trompe l'œil painting. Even a tiny bird painted in realistic detail, with a hint of a shadow, perched on a high shelf, may cause an unsuspecting person to look twice. Other tiny creatures – a butterfly, for example, or a lizard, quietly resting on a wall – can have the same effect.

Domestic animals often figure in the personally significant images that clients ask to have included in a mural. They often wish for some element of their personal life to be incorporated into a composition – details such as a personal portrait, an event from their past or some object or occurrence that relates to their present life. Or they may ask an artist to paint something that is inextricably linked in a humorous or sentimental way to them and to the house or apartment in which the mural is to be painted – and a much-loved family pet is a common request.

Pet dogs and cats are often painted into a themed composition, such as a garden landscape mural, in which, for example, the family's faithful hound is depicted bounding across a lawn or waiting by the garden gate. A pet may be given a place in a painted scene of the family, or depicted as a realistic image on a plain wall. All owners are captivated by the idiosyncrasies of their pets, and a mural that captures a habit or mood of a dog or a cat may be especially endearing to the owner. The realism with which an artist can capture not only the appearance but the expression, body language, and habitual mood of a pet can be delightful.

▶ **A pet terrier** sits watchfully beside an open door. This charming trompe l'œil was painted on the wall of a billiard room in a house in southern England. The dog's owner has a house in Switzerland, where the dog lives; and since the pet cannot accompany him on trips to England, the owner commissioned the mural to remind him of his absent friend.
MURALIST: GRAHAM RUST

The many anecdotes that illustrate how painters have tested the realism of each others' representations always merit retelling. In one, the Roman writer Pliny recounts a tale of rivalry between Zeuxis and Parrhasius, who painted a curtain so convincingly that Zeuxis tried to pull it back. Zeuxis, on the other hand, painted some grapes that so fooled a bird that it tried to peck at them. But when Zeuxis painted a boy holding some grapes, and a bird tried to peck at them, he realized that he had failed in his objective: the boy could not have been painted convincingly because the bird was not afraid of him. Another tale from the thirteenth century recounts how the Florentine painter, Giotto, when apprenticed to Cimabue, painted a fly which Cimabue tried to brush away from the nose of the figure on which it was painted.

At times in the past when trompe l'œil has been in fashion, hunting trophies, such as antlers, game birds, hares, and rabbits, have been painted in trompe l'œil arrangements inside decorative open-fronted cabinets. Modern interpretations have been painted as arrangements of guns and other shooting paraphernalia beside the bagged game on the backs of kitchen or cupboard doors.

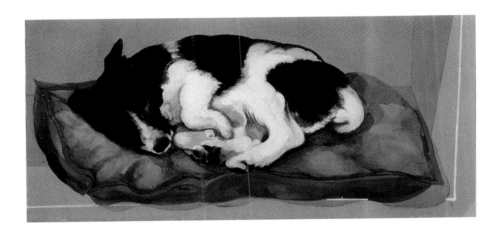

◀ **A pet may be painted** in tender detail in a place where it favours sleeping or sitting – like this puppy captured in paint, eternally asleep on its cushion at the foot of a large trompe l'œil panel in a hallway. Stories of deceptions successfully perpetrated by small trompe l'œil paintings are frequently exaggerated … but, reports the muralist, the real dog was seen to respond to its sleeping counterpart by scratching at the image and lifting its paw.
MURALIST: PETER WHITEMAN

Not all murals are based on the traditional themes that were explored by famous artists of past generations, who perfected in their greatest paintings the techniques of illusion. Muralists know and understand their work, but having studied it, then follow their own ideas in their work. The photographs on the following eight pages illustrate examples of illusionistic murals by leading artists and muralists from several countries, some of whom are celebrated internationally for their work in other media. These works differ widely in size and style, but all contain a surrealistic element.

The mural opposite is based on a traditional subject: a landscape perspective; but this painted landscape is framed by the curling protrusions of the attic wall's torn surface – which appears to be made not of plaster but of a more fragile material, such as canvas or even paper. This device creates an illusory dimension within the room, and beyond it. We are not necessarily fully deceived by the illusion of ripped fabric or canvas through which a landscape can be seen – and perhaps it is not intended that we should be – but the effect it creates has great impact.

Shadows play a very important part in the ability of a trompe l'œil to represent an illusion realistically enough to deceive the eye. On the extreme right of this mural is a small window, through which light is entering the room. The artist has painted the shadows apparently cast toward the left side of the image by the curling edges of the torn wall surface – but the shadows he has painted are far deeper than would really be cast by the light from such a small window. This visual trick dramatically emphasizes the illusion that the torn surface enters the viewer's space within the room and makes the trompe l'œil more credible.

Allowing a fecund imagination free reign to express ideas in a wall painting can have startling results. This is especially likely when trompe l'œil is used to bring fantasies to life. Representing in a mural something that does not exist with the intention of making it seem real is a surrealistic concept; and a trompe l'œil with an intentionally bizarre element adds a dimension to a wall painting. The dimension might be wit or humour, which can alter the messages in the painting and give rise to fascinating new interpretations. In addition, distorting perspectives and using especially vivid or unlikely colours can galvanize the impact of a composition – or just communicate the artist's quirky sense of reality and fun.

A surrealistic trompe l'œil may not fit comfortably into the drawing room, say, of a lovely period house. But a poor conversion may be made to seem more interesting with the addition of an amusing or surprising mural in an unexpected place. Converting the unused space in a loft or basement into an extra bedroom or a work room is common nowadays and these often windowless wall areas are perfect locations for experimenting with new ideas. However, a mural with a surrealistic theme might be most at home on the walls of a room in a modern apartment, house, or public building. With no period features to be considered; its walls offer an open canvas for the realization of startling new ideas.

◄ **This surreal trompe l'œil** treats the blank wall of an attic room as an expansive canvas. The surface appears to have been torn back, revealing beneath it a view of the Loire Valley at Orléans in northern France. Its effect on the enclosed attic room is dramatic: it alters the mood, encouraging viewers to explore beyond the limits of the solid wall into the world beyond. The French artist manipulates space by breaking through the picture plane, as well as into the viewer's space inside the room.
MURALIST: MINT

◄ **An unrealistic perspective** produces an animated fireplace. The famous British artist has created a witty image, in which a quirky reality is imposed by a combination of real and painted objects. Shadows from a falling ornament are positioned unexpectedly in a playful way – while some real objects have been stuck to the wall and shadows added.
MURALIST: DAVID HOCKNEY

► **Paper covered with architectural drawings** is torn open to reveal classical architectural details beneath, flooded with light. Unrelated objects rest on the architecture. Strong shadows define folds in the pale, buff-coloured paper, whose fragility is exquisitely represented. This panel is 72 inches by 48 inches (1.9 metres by 12.7 metres) and is painted in acrylics on canvas.
MURALIST: RICHARD SHIRLEY SMITH

▲ **A profound statement about war** is made in this monumental fresco. The work surrounds an octagonal room, of which three walls are shown here. A painted column in each corner supports the cracked entablure, transforming the room into a rotunda through which the spectator views the landscape. Each section has a different meaning. In this view, the figure on the left represents diplomacy, and the face behind, the helplessness of the onlooker. The columns of green marble represent the weapons of war. In the centre is the fallen head of Man – the dying soldier – and the foot is the oppressor. In front of the sensual face of Mother Earth, a hand points enquiringly to the right, asking who is to blame. The red trompe l'œil curtain symbolizes spilt blood. Out of sight, a landscape representing peace disappears into the sea. The Argentine artist painted this work for his country's embassy in London.
MURALIST: RICARDO CINALLI

Contemporary styles in trompe l'œil reflect the freedom of interpretation and experimentation expressed in the work of artists of the late 1800s and early 1900s, and can be equally exciting and varied. Among the generations of artists who broke away from earlier traditions reaching back to the Florentine artist Giotto (c. 1276–c. 1377) and the early fourteenth century were the surrealists of the 1920s and 1930s. These artists used dreams and chance effects to mingle reason with unreason and create a new reality in art. They attempted to reveal the unconscious through distorted perspectives and the juxtaposition of unlikely objects, or by placing something in an unusual

context. The surrealists delighted in bizarre and extraordinary subject matter. They appreciated illusion in art and revived the art of trompe l'œil for its ability to give unusual subjects an appearance of normality.

Surrealistic murals from the creative imagination of the British artist Lincoln Seligman enliven many public spaces in London. As a barrister at the English bar, he painted as an antidote to stress in his work until, in 1980, he gave up law to paint murals full-time. He quickly progressed to substantial corporate commissions for international clients. Among the better known of his murals are those painted in two London airports, New York's Russian Tea Room, and Asprey in the nearby Trump Tower on Fifth Avenue.

▲ **A bank** is treated – in the words of the artist – as a latter-day temple in this mural. It occupies a wall 10 feet high by 38 feet long (30.5 metres by 116 metres) in the principal lobby of the Swiss Banking Corporation in London. The janitor has swept up his last pile of surplus bank notes and fantasy people arrive, to break

The award-winning work illustrated below was commissioned for the Swiss Bank Corporation's prestigious new London offices beside the River Thames, designed by the British architect Richard Seifert. Seligman's brief was to create a mural that would "show visitors that creativity and a fresh outlook go hand-in-hand with solidity and experience". His stated aim was to link two concepts not normally perceived as compatible: Swiss banking and the idea of fun. His theme for the mural was based on the idea of making it contrast the solidity of the building with the fleeting, inspirational nature of many commercial ideas. The idea behind the mural is that the solid building is

down the building at the end of the day (only to reconstruct it ready for the building to reopen next day). The mural's visual framework is a painted continuation of the lobby's real architecture. It is painted in acrylics on plasterboard at one end of the corporation's huge entrance hall.

MURALIST: LINCOLN SELIGMAN

dismantled at the end of each working day, when the 1,400 or so people who work in it leave, and reassembled in time for their appearance at the start of business on the next day. The assertion of the Irish Anglican bishop and philosopher, George Berkeley (1685–1753), that things can only be said to exist when they are perceived by a mind – and, by extension, may cease to exist when not being perceived – was one inspiration for this idea.

A row of elevators occupying the wall of the lobby at right angles to the mural is mirrored in the painting; this device extends the elevators along the apparent length of the building's main lobby – and it bridges reality and fantasy by blending the real building into the painting.

▲ **Figures peer down** from a painted balcony surrounding what appears to be an opening in the ceiling to a cloudy blue sky. This Renaissance fresco was painted inside the dome of the Palazzo Ducale in Mantua, Italy. Its painted sky may have been the first work of art in which an artist knowingly used perspective and other trompe l'œil techniques to apparently open a ceiling to the heavens.
MURALIST: ANDREA MANTEGNA

The decorative potential of ceilings has been neglected in the twentieth century. In contemporary interior design, ceilings may be included in a room's colour scheme, or be the setting for imaginative lighting; but as a major decorative feature they are largely ignored. It has not always been so. In Europe from early Christian times to the late 1800s, ceilings were a vehicle for works of art. In Christian churches, in civic buildings, and in great houses, the ceiling was always the place for paintings of God, the saints, and heaven.

The fresco reproduced above, by the Early Renaissance artist Andrea Mantegna (c. 1431–1506), is considered a remarkable innovation in illusionistic ceiling painting. Before Mantegna, artists sometimes painted church

◄ **In this simple but spectacular** ceiling trompe l'œil for an Italian restaurant, the artist has painted a sky view through an oculus, an opening traditionally built into a dome. The tubs of orange trees in the bottom corners reveal that Mantegna's influential painting (opposite) was the muralist's main inspiration. It is painted on a ceiling above a spiral staircase with its base abutting a flat wall. Instead of peering down from the oculus into the dimness of the world, however, the bird in the detail below is in flight.
MURALISTS: DAVIES, KEELING, TROWBRIDGE

vaults blue and dotted them with stars to look like the heavens. But Mantegna's fresco was the first in which an artist consciously tried to make the roof seem to open directly to Heaven. It marks the start of an era in which the effects of perspective were explored with dramatic results.

Ceilings decorated with magnificent illusionistic paintings became an integral part of the interior design of buildings of the 1700s and 1800s, the centuries that saw the emergence of the styles art historians later named Baroque and Rococo. Baroque architects sought to involve the viewer emotionally in their buildings, in which painting, sculpture, dramatic lighting effects, colour, and movement were united with the architecture. The Baroque

period began in Rome in the early 1600s, and spread to other Roman Catholic European states. During the Catholic counter-reformation the rulers of these states encouraged the building of new churches, and artists were commissioned to paint vast, allegorical frescoes on the ceilings. One such ceiling was painted by Pietro da Cortona (1596–1669), an architect-painter, one of the leaders of the Baroque style. His illusionistic fresco on the ceiling of the Barberini Palace in Rome depicts figures seemingly floating in and out of an imaginary opening in the sky.

In France, Baroque evolved into the more sophisticated, less grandiose Rococo style, of which the magnificent gilded and painted ceiling of the Hall of Mirrors at Versailles, near Paris, is perhaps the apogee. The name "rococo" comes from the French rocaille or "shell", for shells were a common motif in Rococo decoration. Rococo spread, in its turn, outward from France.

The culmination of these great illusionistic traditions was the work of the Venetian painter Giovanni Battista Tiepolo (c. 1692–1770), who decorated the ceiling of the Residenz at Würzburg in Franconia. His frescoes were a final touch of magnificence for the splendid new palace of the wealthy prince-bishops of this Catholic state in what is now southern Germany. Tiepolo's themes were less extravagant than those of his predecessors, his colours more subdued, and natural light played a major role in his ceilings.

Ceilings in the tradition of the 1600s and 1700s are still occasionally commissioned. One example is Graham Rust's *The Temptation of Christ* at Ragley Hall (see page 88), an English country mansion whose interior is largely the work of the English Baroque architect James Gibbs (1682–1754).

Skies also make appropriate subjects for ceiling paintings in less grand homes. Sky is an obvious theme for adding height to a low ceiling simply because blue is a colour that seems to recede. A high ceiling in an old building can accommodate more elaborate effects. Indeed, a ceiling above a staircase is an interesting area for an effective trompe l'œil, as its distance from the viewer adds to its effect.

A ceiling painting of a sky can be effective in other ways. Opening a section of ceiling with a painted skylight, through which pale sky can be seen, can give an impression of space and light above, add interest to an unadorned space, and make an attractive focal point. Again, painting an entire ceiling to show a broad expanse of blue summer sky with soft hints of white clouds may bring a fresh, light feeling into a room. Mouldings, where they exist, can become the framework of such a celestial composition.

Ceiling space is suited to a variety of decorative themes. Simulated ornate plasterwork is common and looks elegant. Alternatively, a mural painted on a wall might extend onto the ceiling. In children's rooms especially, where fantasy is always appreciated, mythical characters in allegorical settings painted on ceilings could open a world of dreams.

Painting overhead can be exhausting and uncomfortable, and the scaffolding and ladders required can be inconvenient, so painting on canvas in a studio and attaching the finished canvas to the ceiling is a great advantage.

◀ **The trick** of achieving a stunning impact with a minimum of detail is illustrated in this modern mural painted on the lobby ceiling of a European hotel. A peacock on the circular balcony (a framing device seen in the first trompe l'œil ceilings of the early 1600s, and often used since) looks up into the blue sky, where a swallow is winging its way below the clouds. The colours in this mural are tastefully echoed in the decor of the hotel lobby.
MURALISTS: RICHMOND INTERNATIONAL

Muralists are often required to simulate in their wall paintings a variety of building materials, such as marble or wood. In recent years there has been an explosion of interest in decorating walls and furniture with paint effects, such as sponging, ragging, dragging, and stippling. The techniques of marbling and wood graining are also often thought of as paint effects, but they really fall into a different category. They are more specialized techniques, whose role is to deceive the eye. Applied with artistic flair, they play the role of a trompe l'œil beautifully.

Faux marbre, or false marble, has a long history. Panels of simulated rare marbles were common in the frescoes found in houses in the Roman city of Pompeii. Today, they are still often used to decorate small areas, but they can also be painted over entire walls or other surfaces – muralists can use *faux marbre* to transform plastered walls or uninteresting floors into illusions of expensive, polished marble.

The different marbles that occur naturally vary widely in colour and design. Their swirling patterns and irregular veinings can be subtle or bold, and their colours range from the pale grays of white marble to the golds and yellows of sienna marble and the rich green of malachite. An artist might imitate one of the many real marbles or simply invent a marble.

Simulated marble may be painted either as inlays on selected areas, or in slabs or blocks, or as patterns made up of combinations of square and rectangular shapes of differing colours. Such decorative devices can add an air of distinguished elegance to any interior, but are especially suitable for living rooms, bathrooms, lobbies, and entrance halls.

Marbling and woodgraining may be incorporated into murals wherever appropriate – to make a column or a balustrade look as if it were really made of marble, for example, or on a door or an item of furniture. Alternatively they may both be used to cover a whole floor or wall.

The techniques of distressing can be used to make fresh paintwork look naturally faded and worn. It can be applied to produce a variety of effects, from soft, washed-out colours to a weatherbeaten appearance. Murals painted to simulate ancient wall paintings and frescoes are sometimes distressed after the painting is finished to give an impression of authenticity.

Artists may use any number of techniques for distressing painted surfaces. After colour has been applied to the wall and has dried, it may be sanded off, scraped away, or rubbed back to highlight imperfections beneath the paint and turn any cracks and lumps into features. Each artist tends to favour a particular method, using sandpaper, a wire brush, or wire wool. Darker colours may be allowed to run into cracks in the wall, then the surplus remaining on the surface is rubbed off. The result of employing distressing techniques is to make the bright paint colours glow rather more softly, as if after centuries of weathering. To achieve a thoroughly worn look, an artist may block out parts of a painting so that chunks of plaster seem to be missing.

Distressing also refers to the technique of breaking up the ground (base coat) for marbling to create different textured effects – the first coat of

paint is subjected to any number of different treatments before drying. Rags, sponges, brushes, even old newspaper may be used to break up the original brushstrokes and create the desired textured effect on the wet paint.

Over the last decade, a fashion has emerged for distressing surfaces of all types – doors, window frames, furniture and floors, as well as doors. The aim is sometimes to achieve an informal look or a particular atmosphere, or just to maximize the impression of wear and tear.

▲ **In this fresco** from a house in Pompeii, architectural motifs, such as columns and friezes, frame panels in which a painting of figures and buildings looks like a picture hanging on the wall. The Romans used a wide palette of colours, of which this scarlet – called Pompeian red – was the most popular.
MUSEO NAZIONALE, NAPLES

◀ **The entire lobby** of the Chestnut Place apartment building in Chicago is covered by this trompe l'œil mural scheme, inspired by the lovely Romanesque Church of San Miniato al Monte in Florence, Italy. The mural is composed of classical architectural devices, such as columns, pediments, and Roman arches, plus panels and geometric patterns, all traced with *faux* marbling. The mural covers walls and floor, so that windows and doorways leading into the lobby become part of the mural.

MURALIST: RICHARD HAAS

◄ **The geometric outlines** of the panels on the wall in the background of this photograph are softened by the delicate veining of the *faux marbre* – orange on yellow, white on orange and on black, and black and white on gray. The walls of both rooms are beautifully sectioned by the clean black lines of the painted dado rails, which link the separate spaces and coordinate the different elements of the decor.
MURALISTS: MIMI O'CONNELL AND PETER FARLOW

◄ **The decoration of Roman town houses in Pompeii** was the inspiration for this room. The artist has painted false windows, typical of those found in Roman houses, on either side of the bust. Wall panels are framed with *faux* onyx, and some contain medallions, garlands, and other decorative devices. The artist successfully simulated the lustrous Pompeian red, and then distressed the wall to give an aged effect.
MURALIST: CHRISTOPHER DREW

◀ **The elegant proportions** of this Georgian room are complemented by a harmonious decor inspired by classical architectural elements. Realistic Ionic pilasters blend with real niches on either side of the fireplace. Above it, the artist has painted a relief sculpture framed by an arch; a simulated crack across the pediment enhances its authenticity. A symmetrical composition is formed by the alignment of the niches with the monochrome relief panels, complete with trompe l'œil painted frames beneath the frieze, and the panels of gray *faux marbre* below the dado rail.

MURALIST: ALAN DODD

▲ **Trompe l'œil** appears to conquer the limitations of this interior space by revealing an illusion of sky through a vision of a ruined ceiling. The top storey of a pyramidal tower in Italy has been treated with ornate decoration intended to simulate decay on the tower's vaulted ceiling. Paint has created a false wall of stone blocks, their corners apparently chipped and worn.
MURALIST: RENZO MONGIARDINO

The fashion of the last decade for making interiors look antique or merely less than impeccable by distressing painted and other surfaces has inspired some ingenious muralists to extend the boundaries of trompe l'œil still further, by painting architectural fragments and images of broken plaster, stone, and brick onto walls and ceilings. These unusual effects are sometimes introduced into a mural as details, to suggest the ruined interior of another age, perhaps, or to create a strange, surrealistic atmosphere. They are sometimes also used on a large scale, in the form of a broken wall or ceiling, for example, to alter the visual impression of a room's architecture. Some of the most convincing trompe l'œil tricks are carried off by representing an extra dimension on a wall, such as a layer of broken architectural fabric revealing another layer beneath. The wealth of possibilities presented by these trompe l'œil conceits seems almost limitless. They can wreak amazing transformations in an interior.

These two pages illustrate an extraordinary example of a building where this has been done. La Torre, a lookout tower built in the 1500s by Spanish invaders on the coast of southern Tuscany in Italy, was converted by the Italian architect Renzo Mongiardino into a second home for its owner, the jewellery designer Elsa Peretti.

With the imaginative use of trompe l'œil, Mongiardino transformed this military complex of pokey guard rooms, awkward, winding staircases, and arrow-slit windows into a fantasy retreat, using paint to alter visually the interior architecture and atmosphere of the building. The artist covered the ground-floor living room in trompe l'œil frescoes. He also employed devices such as false windows apparently looking out onto sunny landscapes, painted stone blocks, and simulated ornamental stucco to radically alter the appearance of small rooms and dark stairwells.

In a historic building, where a desire to preserve the original may rule out rebuilding, trompe l'œil may be a practical way of overcoming structural limitations. The architecture of any interior can be made to look completely different at considerably less cost than would be needed to rebuild.

◀ **A painted wooden shutter** is left open for the light to shine in, illuminating thick walls painted in warm, sunny tones. It seems to let a breath of air into what is in reality the enclosed, narrow, steep stairwell of a sixteenth-century tower in Italy. Below the false window, aged, broken stucco appears to have peeled away to reveal the stone structure beneath, complete with a few weeds growing through. Any area of esthetic weakness, like this stairwell, can be transformed with skill and original, intriguing ideas.
MURALIST: RENZO MONGIARDINO

In any trompe l'œil a muralist may need to represent any number of natural materials, especially wood, and manufactured materials, such as textiles and carpets. Drapes and curtains, tapestry and rugs have all been simulated in paint; and woodgraining – or *faux bois* – has been an established tradition in interior design for centuries. It was especially popular during the 1800s.

Today, woodgraining is commonly incorporated into trompe l'œils. A table, for instance, or chairs, may be part of a composition and must be woodgrained to look authentic. Trompe l'œil doorways, cupboards, cabinets, shelves, and bookcases all need to be woodgrained. Alternatively, woodgraining may be used alone, to line a wall with false panelling, for example.

Wood effects can be applied directly to turn doors and panels made of inexpensive woods, such as whitewood or new pine, into something that looks more prepossessing. Painting the surface with a simulation of a rare or costly wood is an esthetic solution to the problem of inelegant wood substitutes, such as plywood, MDF, and other boardings, and it can be cheaper than buying wood and having the door or panelling made by hand.

Beautiful wood is increasingly costly, and some hardwoods are now very rarely available, but the grained, polished surfaces of woods that have been popular in the past, such as rosewood or walnut, can be simulated to perfection by a talented muralist. A browse through catalogues will reveal lovely rare woods suited to every decor style.

Many of the hardwoods traditionally used for furniture are now scarcely available from sustainable sources, so woodgraining is an environmentally considerate solution to the problem of conservation. Brazilian mahogany is one example. The traditional use for the wood of this rainforest tree, with its warm, reddish brown tone and decorative graining, has been for quality cabinet work and distinctive joinery, and it makes superb panelling, skirting board, doors, and cupboards. Woodgraining can be applied over entire wall surfaces. The rich, light-brown European oak and the gray and cream American white oak are ideal subjects for this type of application.

Faux drapes and tapestries were often used to decorate early Christian churches, and trompe l'œil wallpaper depicting heavy swags of rich fabrics were used in the 1800s in Europe and America. These days, curtains have a role in many locations and situations: as heavy swags of rich velvet, seemingly pulled back to reveal a mural or a real picture, perhaps, beneath. A heavy velvet curtain held open with ornate cords can give a mural a theatrical effect. Alternatively, drapes may be left to hang mysteriously closed, concealing anything that captures the viewer's imagination.

Painted fabrics can also cover entire walls – and more. A room might be painted to look like a tent, with fabric gathered at a central point in a ceiling, draped over false poles at the tops of the walls, and falling to the floor in soft folds. The effect of such a scheme is one of cosy intimacy. Alternatively, *faux* textiles may play a minor role in a decor. A blind might be painted in a trompe l'œil window, for instance. The visual effect can be as stunning if a rug or a sumptuous carpet is painted on a floor. Eastern rugs

◄ **False pine woodgraining** gives this large, octagonal entrance hall of a private house a distinguished appearance. The wooden mouldings are real; the artist painted the space in between them, and finished the surfaces with a scumble glaze. This painted panelling invests the room with the warmth and luxury of a wood-lined room at far less expense than buying the wood and having it installed would entail.
MURALIST: ROBERT O'DEA

◄ **An impressive dining room** furnished in period style has walls decorated with trompe l'œil fabric. The mural extends the real curtains across the wall, softening its flat surface and enveloping the whole room in opulent yellow textile. The muralist has captured the tactile quality of the soft, silken fabric, whose sensuous, painted folds complement and harmonize with the room's luxurious ambience.
VEERE GRENNEY ASSOCIATES

and carpets can be costly, but a painted one might be more affordable, and when it wears it will only need retouching with a paintbrush.

Rugs can also be painted as wall hangings, as can tapestries. These are old and fascinating subjects for trompe l'œils, presenting many thematic possibilities. To depict a tapestry realistically, it is hardly necessary for the muralist to indicate depth, except, maybe, for a curled corner throwing a shadow on the wall beneath.

▲ **A mosaic panel from Pompeii** inspired this trompe l'œil panel. The Roman mosaic was composed of a collection of fish and octopuses eating a sea creature depicted in the centre. This composition has more variety and avoids the stark realism of its predecessor, and its atmosphere is much more tranquil. The muralist chose a mythological sea creature for the centrepiece.
MURALIST: CAROLINE COWLEY

Simulating mosaics is an unusual application of trompe l'œil. As decoration for interiors, mosaics can be traced to the ancient Greeks, who used roughly shaped cubes of coloured stone, called tesserae, to make patterned floors. Wealthy Romans copied this practice, so that, like wall paintings, mosaic floors, walls, and ceilings enhanced the prestige of a household. They became fashionable throughout the Roman Empire. Roman artesans developed the art of mosaic, laying floors in beautiful patterns, and using tesserae to compose pictures as detailed as paintings, including complex figurative scenes. They recycled old and used materials, making their floors from fragments of glass and tile, as well as stone.

The theme of a mosaic in a Roman room might indicate the room's function. For example, a mosaic floor depicting fish might possibly be laid in a dining room. Roman artists, who loved the art of illusion, also tried to

▲ **The sea creatures** in the trompe l'œil panel on the left are depicted in fine detail, as the enlargement below reveals. The panel, on a bathroom wall, surrounded by marble and mirrors, is 59 inches high and 61 inches wide (about 1.5 metres square). The muralist painted the tesserae to the scale of the Roman original.
MURALIST: CAROLINE COWLEY

create trompe l'œil in mosaic. A surviving example from the second century A.D., called *The Unswept Floor,* depicts scattered remnants of fish bones, shellfish, and other debris, with suggested shadows outlining their forms.

In twentieth-century interiors, simulated mosaics might be painted as small panels of simple, geometric patterns on the walls of bathrooms or kitchens. For inspiration, muralists might turn to the surviving examples from Greece or Rome, which used a small range of blended colours, or the glorious tradition of mosaic art of the Byzantine Empire, where artesans used a rich palette of stones, including gold, silver, and other metallic colours. The English Arts and Crafts movement at the turn of the twentieth century revived the art of mosaics, and the walls and ceilings of some notable buildings were decorated with beautiful mosaic compositions, which provide another source of ideas for muralists today.

Paint is still often used to bring colour and interest to floors, especially concrete floors, which might be given a mosaic pattern, or painted to look like old, faded tiles. The potential themes are endless. For ideas for tiles, artists can tap the heritage of the Islamic Empire, from the beautiful peacock-blue glazed tiles that decorate the domes of Persian mosques to the blue tiles, called *azulejos,* of southern Spain.

◄ *Faux marbre* was the theme chosen for this mural. It depicts trompe l'œil segments of broken terrazzo, a type of paving made of tiny chips of broken marble set in cement, in warm colours, in a wall of distressed plaster. False marble effects such as these are just as suitable for floors, and even for small surfaces, such as table or cupboard tops, window ledges, stairs, and steps, as they are for large wall surfaces.
MURALIST: ROBERT O'DEA

◄ **The arches** of *The Cloister*, as this mural, in the entrance hall of a private house, is entitled, are painted as if they follow on from the real arch in the foreground, increasing the illusion of depth. Daylight appears to penetrate the mural from an implied space on the right. The plinth bearing a vase of flowers on the wall ahead arrests the eye and confirms that this is where the "wall" ends. Above it, a small aperture suggests open space beyond.
MURALIST: COLIN FAILES

▲ **A chequered floor** dramatically emphasizes and extends the visual space of this room across two apparently adjoining rooms. The window in the distance continues the illusion of space to the urban architecture outside. The artist has effectively altered the structure of this building, creating a distinguished entrance on a featureless wall, from which the pediments crowning the successive doorways lead the eye into the serene illusion of other rooms. The now-famous American muralist painted this doorway in 1974 on the wall of his Greene Street studio New York, but the work was destroyed in 1982.
MURALIST: RICHARD HAAS

Doorways opening into visions of rooms ahead are beguiling, even mislead-ing, at their most realistic. Fictional space takes the eye into a mysterious world it cannot enter. The trompe l'œil illusion of repeated arches, doorways, or other openings has a magical fascination like that of a Russian doll, which can be pulled apart to reveal another, smaller doll, and then another, each one diminishing in size. A trompe l'œil on this theme may be intended to deceive, but it is more likely to astonish a person seeing it for the first time, until a second glance confirms the clever trick.

A mural showing an enfilade, or succession, of doorways receding into the distance has a theatrical quality, which may be heightened by light pene-trating the composition from the hidden rooms on either side of each doorway. Glimpses of different furnishings and furniture in each successive room may give the painting a slightly strange atmosphere. The Dutch painter, Jan Vermeer (1632–75), often painted rooms with doorways through which other rooms can be seen. Their calm, dreamlike atmosphere has inspired several muralists to create wall paintings on a similar theme.

The two examples illustrated above have an atmosphere of quietude; the contained space at the end of each enfilade is within sight, but will always remain impenetrable, except in the viewer's imagination.

▶ **A succession of doorways**
leading into other rooms is
suggested in this trompe l'œil,
which brings light and depth to
a hallway in a narrow town
house. Soft light filters into the
rooms from windows out of
view to the side. A gilded mirror
that hangs on the wall of the
real room is reflected in the
mural. This mural is painted in
oils directly onto the surface of
a blank wall inside a real door
frame. Gold leaf was applied to
the mirror frame and to the
console table in the mural.
MURALIST: SOPHIA BARRATT

Many buildings have rooms with a door giving onto a corridor, from which, in turn, a door leads into another room. Painting an enfilade – a succession – of doors leading from room to room therefore tends to give the impression that the viewer is in a grand building – or even in a large rustic building, where rooms lead on, one into another.

As is true of most trompe l'œil murals, however, false doorways are most effective when the muralist has designed a scheme that is sympathetic to the architecture of the room or hallway, and which harmonizes with the decor. An example of a scheme in which the illusion and the real room link well is illustrated on page 119; here the muralist painted a reflection of an extension of rooms she may have designed had she been the architect.

To deceive the eye of the viewer effectively, a false doorway must be seen head on. It is therefore important that the mural be positioned on a wall directly opposite the doorway through which people enter the room. The mural on page 119, painted for a narrow town house, fulfils these criteria very effectively. On entering the house, people walk into a hallway, and as they turn left into the first room, the mural is on the wall directly ahead.

False doorways are appropriate in several interior situations. Some hall-ways or corridors end abruptly at a blank wall, and this end wall is a worthy place in which to paint an illusion of continued space. Others take a turn at the end to the left or the right, so that a blank wall faces anyone walking along it toward the turning. In an apartment or a small house these hallways are often quite narrow. Treating the end wall with an illusion of space ahead can lend light and depth – and add a beautiful mural – to what is often a dark corner. From the vantage point of distance, at the other end of the passageway, the illusion of space ahead can be very deceptive, and the mural painted in the fictional space through the wall can lend colour and interest to the real world of the onlooker.

A room or a corridor with a single door on one side may appear unbalanced. Painting another door at the opposite end can bring symmetry to the architecture, restoring harmony to the room and creating an impression of space where there is none.

Creating doors and windows where none exist is a continuing theme in the repertoire of trompe l'œil subjects. The windowless walls of internal bathrooms are popular areas for creating false windows. A mural in such a situation might peek into the enclosed space of a secret room, with mysterious furniture projecting from hidden corners, tantalizingly out of view.

◄ **A trompe l'œil** is at its most effective when viewed from directly ahead, so that the flat wall surface is not clearly visible and does not spoil the illusion. This mural, called *The West Wing*, has a certain grandeur. It is a highly elaborate illusion, in which doorways alternate in a succession of images, each revealing a different room with ornate decoration and period furniture. The painted panelling on the left side of the mural continues all the way round the room. The mural was painted for an exhibition, where the moveable screen in front of it was also exhibited. To its surface are attached canvas panels painted in acrylics with trompe l'œil woodgraining, a style that blends well with the mural. After the exhibition the mural was dismantled and installed in an interior.
MURALIST: ROBERTA GORDON-SMITH

◄ **A false niche** is apparently carved out of the flat surface of a wall devoid of architectural features. The artist has painted the niche and the walls around it in a beautiful representation of the texture of sandstone. Soft shadows mould the niche's shallow depth and cast on its back wall outlines of the bird and the urn on which it perches, the violin, and the music score, which represent the owner's interest in music.
MURALIST: IAN CAIRNIE

▶ **An elegant vase** placed casually on a stack of well-used books creates a fascinating area of interest in this painted niche. Scattered around the books are mementoes – a card, bundles of letters, a scrolled document. This is one of a pair of trompe l'œil niches painted on either side of a door in the entrance hall of an ambassador's apartment – the other is shown in the photograph opposite.

MURALIST: IAN CAIRNIE

▲ **A neoclassical trompe l'œil niche** housing a classical urn interrupts the vertical plane of this room in an old country house in Majorca, Spain. The trompe l'œil stonework merges into the real stone wall, and the urn casts credible shadows on the back of the niche. An empty wine glass left on the ledge, an old book propped against the urn's base, contradict the formality of the painting. A clutter of objects on a table in front gives this photograph the appearance and atmosphere of a still-life composition.
MURALIST: FELIX DE CADENAS

The impact a mural can make on an interior can be very powerful, so that a small room might easily be overwhelmed by a mural covering a whole wall. Conversely, a small wall painting can form a focal point in a room. The trompe l'œil niche is an old decorative device that has been in fashion time and again throughout European history. Using paint and perspective to give an impression of shallow depth was common in Pompeian interiors at the end of the first millennium B.C. (see page 107). False niches were first used in the 16th century to decorate European palaces and churches, and since then they have been a popular decorative feature in domestic and public buildings. Traditionally, they contained trompe l'œil busts and statues rendered *en grisaille* (a French term, meaning 'in gray') to achieve an effect of imitation stone or marble. To paint a realistic-looking bust or statue in grisaille work, an artist would usually use several tones of gray.

There may be several possible locations for a trompe l'œil niche in a house, depending on whether subtlety or impact is the desired effect. A single niche centred in a wall might create a focal point or simply add interest to a windowless and doorless wall in a small lobby, a small living room, or even a bathroom. Two niches symmetrically placed can have strong decorative impact on a long, featureless wall – in a hallway, perhaps, or either side of a fireplace. Alternatively, a small, delicately painted niche can bring a dark corner of a room to life.

Niches are often painted with the classical rounded arch, but really they can take any form: that of a pointed, horseshoe, or scalloped arch; square, or rectangular, pyramidal, or irregular in shape.

Objects such as the traditional urn or statue, are usually painted inside a trompe l'œil niche. The niche might contain a representation of some famous work of art copied from a museum piece, or some priceless porcelain objet. A false niche is as much a vehicle for typical trompe l'œil trickery and humour as is a wide expanse of wall, so that some small ornament having escaped its daily dusting, a single book leaning against the illusory depth of a shadowed recess in which the silvery threads of a cobweb have been painted slightly above arm's reach, might be appropriate and engaging details.

Rather than stand a single, beautiful work of art on the false base of a niche in the classical manner, a muralist might paint a clutter of everyday objects. The niche's ledge might be strewn with articles of clothing – a hat or a scarf – familiar to the owner; a bag might be tossed carelessly onto it, suggesting someone's recent presence. An assortment of books or beautiful objets d'art might be scattered in disarray there, apparently waiting to be picked up and admired, or dusted and rearranged. Light falling on the collection from a suggested nearby window might pick out certain items from the collection – making the casual observer look twice – or cast their shadows against the back of the niche. An artist can give the objects inside a painted niche the quality of a still-life painting within their illusory setting.

A niche furnished with a vase of flowers or a pot plant is sometimes painted on the chimney boards fitted across the front of disused fireplaces to close them off, or to conceal the fireplace opening during the summer. These boards, also called fireplace panels or *devants de cheminée*, were used in the 1700s in Europe to cover hearths in town and country houses. Today, such paintings, which were traditionally executed for very practical reasons, can be welcome decorative additions to period or modern rooms with open fireplaces. A muralist might use in the painting any of the ideas commonly seen on fire surrounds, simulating relief carvings, the designs in cast ironwork, or pretty tiles or brickwork.

Real alcoves and other recessed spaces can, of course, be painted with trompe l'œil. For example, cupboards or false shelves might be painted in a rectangular recessed area, and might hold books in a disorderly profusion, or neatly ranged ornaments. Devising a trompe l'œil for an awkwardly shaped recessed space is the type of challenge that muralists enjoy.

▲ **The delicate foliage** of a trailing ivy spills through a break in the wall of a niche, which gives a glimpse of sky. On the ledge of the broken niche stands a damaged terracotta urn, its form repeated in the shape of the teapot placed on the top of a wall cupboard. This illusory scene, a detail of a mural which covers all the walls of a private dining room, may become an interesting talking point for guests at dinner.
MURALIST: JONATHAN BRUNSKILL

In the Low Countries in the late 1600s and during the 1700s, artists painted letter holders with notes and odd scraps of correspondence pinned in haphazard arrangements, or ephemera apparently hanging from the surface. This unlikely tradition spread from there to countries that had trading and other ties with the Low Countries, especially to Spain, France, and England.

Later, in the early 1800s, American artists painted still-lifes reminiscent of this, by then established Dutch tradition, with criss-crossed tape pinned to a background of scuffed or marked wood. Stuffed behind this webbing they painted crumpled or folded banknotes, playing cards, pieces of string hanging from nails, and all manner of other objects which, apparently, had some reference to people's everyday life.

This long-established tradition often reappears in modern murals. A collection of tickets or book matches, paper cuttings, or old letters might seem strange subject matter for a trompe l'œil, but they make the most fascinating of themes. In an appropriate setting – a letter rack, or pinned to a painted board – they convey a startling realism, suggesting a three-dimensional illusion of items on a real board, rather than something that extends back, beyond the wall.

Unusual murals like these arouse curiosity. On closer inspection they reveal an inventory of someone's life. An old opera or theatre ticket, a menu from a favourite restaurant, a receipt for an expensive luxury, a printed invitation . . . the variety of possible contents of such a mural is legion and the double illusion of reality and deception makes a captivating visual image. In a contemporary home, a painted letter holder or a pinboard might be hung with personal mementoes, such as postcards, letters, or paintings and drawings by young children. These odds and ends seem bizarre subjects for display, but as a personal trompe l'œil mural in a kitchen, a bedroom, or a study, they hold cherished personal memories of special people and events.

The play of light and shadow, combined with an exquisite rendering of the subject matter, is essential for the trompe l'œil effect to be convincing, for in such a painting the illusion of deep perspective is lost very quickly when the viewer perceives the flatness of the wall surface. If the artist has employed a limited or shallow depth of field, however, the degree of realism that can be achieved with a three-dimensional illusion can be stunning.

Paintings like these can be so small they can occupy a space in which a framed print or photograph might be hung. The artist might treat the background wall surface with a woodgrain effect, or with a colour to match surrounding or nearby surfaces.

A small, intimate trompe l'œil might also be painted on a door or on the front of a cupboard. In this situation, some object representing a hobby or a personal interest, such as a fishing rod or a football shirt for the door of a boy's room, might be most appropriate. A collection of objects hanging from a peg or a hook can be unexpectedly amusing, just because they can be made to look very real, their painted shadows contributing to the illusion.

▶ **A trompe l'œil noticeboard** is reminiscent of Flemish paintings of the 1600s. Tucked behind the webbing is a collection of memorabilia, an inventory of a person's daily existence: crumpled, folded papers, a dog-eared card, an open cheque, a card with a Matisse print. This mural, 24 inches high and 17 inches wide (0.6 metres by 0.4 metres) is painted in oils on canvas. It is one of a series, part of a private collection. It could hang on a wall, but one could also imagine it painted on the front of a cupboard.
MURALIST: STEPHEN ROBERTS

◀ **The contents of this cupboard,** painted life-size, are clearly visible through the unglazed door. The muralist has created a drama of light and shade, carefully detailing the objects inside the cupboard. The card pinned to the shelf, called a cartellino, gives the artist's initials and the date when the mural was painted. The fly resting on the mug – enlarged in the detail above – is a common motif in trompe l'œil, and is a symbol of mortality. It gives the painting an extra dimension of reality.

MURALIST: STEPHEN ROBERTS

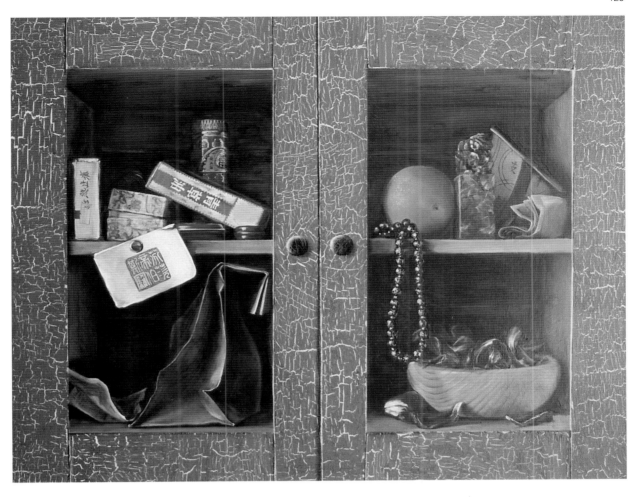

To deceive the eye, a trompe l'œil object must be convincing. It must therefore be painted life-size, or to an accurate scale, so that it looks realistic. The English muralist Stephen Roberts holds a prestigious award for his designs for objets d'art, and he meets all these criteria beautifully in his painting illustrated opposite. He brings a delicate touch to the collection of objects in the cupboard. The light on the objects contrasts with the dark background, suggesting depth so convincingly that the artist has not needed to use perspective devices in the painting.

The shadowy depths and the contents of the cupboard convey an illusion of space beyond the flat wall – making a clear contrast with the small slip of paper pinned to a shelf. This gives the impression of something projecting into the space occupied by the observer. Paper with printing or handwriting tempts anyone who sees it to take a closer look. Slips of paper like this are called cartellinos. They have made regular appearances in trompe l'œil painting since the 1500s. They often carry the artist's signature, or an inscription. In contemporary trompe l'œil, a cartellino might be a dog-eared printed business card bearing the artist's name and telephone number. It can be treated visually in any number of ways – but it is usually painted standing out clearly in the foreground.

▲ **The surface of this cupboard,** just 12 inches high and 16 inches wide (0.3 metres by 0.4 metres), is painted to look like crackled lacquering. Among the objects informally displayed inside are purchases made by the owner from a Chinese supermarket before the painting was begun. The muralist used them to give the work a Chinese theme and has replaced the traditional cartellino with a seal of the type used by Chinese artists.
MURALIST: STEPHEN ROBERTS

▶ **This elegant vitrine,** a trompe l'œil glass-fronted display cabinet in period style, is painted in acrylics on canvas. It was pasted on the wall of a guests' bathroom in a private house. The shelves are filled with delicate china figures, old glass, and objets d'art – a request of the American client. They are representations of the owner's family heirlooms. The beading and other woodwork are carefully detailed.
MURALIST: GARTH BENTON

Realistic cupboards and cabinets, their shelves apparently filled with ornaments, and sets of false shelves displaying beautiful objets d'art, were popular subjects for trompe l'œil in past centuries and continue to have a place in the repertoire of mural artists today. It can be fun planning to fill such cupboards with a coveted collection of rare porcelain, priceless antique ornaments, or colourful bric à brac. A cupboard may brim with a pageant of possessions, from keepsakes to kitsch to collectables: unusual tins or boxes; holiday souvenirs; cups and trophies. The contents might be formally ordered, prettily displayed, or jumbled in fascinating disarray. A trompe l'œil cupboard might take the place of a picture on a living room wall, or bring a hidden corner or an uninteresting wall to life.

◄ **This trompe l'œil bookcase** and the cupboard below it are painted over a door in the library of a Victorian house. The dado rail and the cornice are real. The bookcase is represented as a door to the future: on the top shelf is an apple, symbolizing knowledge, and a pomegranate cut in half, symbolizing time. A mouse's tail projects from between the books on the third shelf – a memorial to a mouse in residence in the room when the owners moved in.
MURALIST: SEBASTIAN WAKEFIELD

Book-filled shelves make decorative trompe l'œil murals and they can be an ingenious, illusionistic solution to the problem of how to disguise obtrusive fixtures or unbalanced features in a room. Simple or sumptuous, on a grand or an intimate scale, they are always enchanting, highly individual works of art.

A wall may be lined with simulated shelves on which faux books are displayed, carefully painted bookcases, or even a trompe l'œil library. Aged and well-read volumes might be ranged, tightly packed in rows or stacked in horizontal piles, with their titles and the names of erudite authors in gold on their worn leather spines. Alternatively, modern paperbacks and hardbacks with colourful jackets, printed with amusing or witty titles and friends' names as authors, might support each other haphazardly.

focus

on details

A close-up look at the plants, animals, and other decorative details and stylized designs and motifs which feature widely in the work of contemporary muralists.

▼ **Playful designs** composed of simple, colourful stylized motifs may be used to coordinate woodwork, walls, and furniture. The clear outlines and bright colours of the fish and flower motifs in this example are emphasized by the intricacy of the pattern, and its darker outlines.

▼ **This trailing ivy**, a design suggested by a false ivy fashioned from red silk which decorated the client's room, and the leaves and branches of other plants seen protruding through the painted brickwork allude to plant life burgeoning beyond the wall.
MURALIST: ANTHONY KOWALSKI

▲ **A vine bearing a profusion of leaves** twists and winds between wall and ceiling. The artist has painted its intense colours and strong foreground detail against a background of pale sky and the neutral shades of painted stonework, uniting trompe l'œil effects with real architecture.

▲ **The contrasting hues of flowers** make splashes of colour in the foreground of this garden, framed by steps and railings leading up to a pergola. The tones of the flower beds diminish toward the background and merge into the misty grays of a city view.
MURALIST: MARIE BYNG

▼ **Floral designs** can be used to make precise but flowing patterns for decorative murals. This example, inspired by French paintings on wooden panels, is precise and formal but ornate, its symmetry serving to highlight the design of the central motif.
MURALIST: IAN CAIRNIE

▼ **The decorative leaves and flowers** of this detail were inspired by ancient hangings from India's Coromandel coast, depicting an early tree of life. The originals arrived in Europe in the 1600s in consignments of silks and painted fabrics carried by ships engaged in the spice trade.
MURALIST: CAROLINE COWLEY

▲ **A vase brimming with freshly cut flowers,** painted in eye-deceiving detail, makes a colourful display in a trompe l'œil niche painted in *faux* woodgraining. The shadows cast by the vase and the flowers on the back of the niche establish its shallow depth.
MURALIST: GARTH BENTON

▲ **Exquisite compositions** of flowers and leaves in harmonizing colours can be assembled into beautiful patterns for decorative murals, as in this detail from a mural inspired by an eighteenth-century chinoiserie design at Château Haroué in Alsace-Lorraine, France.
MURALISTS: IAN CAIRNIE AND TONY RAYMOND

136

▼ **These *faux* relief wood carvings** are exquisitely painted to resemble finger plates. The trompe l'œil portrays a fascinating, three-dimensional study of seashells.
MURALIST: IAN CAIRNIE

▼ **This marble panel** with relief carvings is a trompe l'œil painted above a bath of real marble. The design was inspired by the frieze carved on the Parthenon on the Acropolis in Athens.

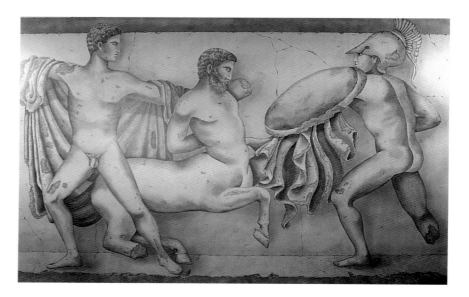

▲ **Effects both subtle and stunning** may be achieved by painting relief decorations in real or false panels. Seashells of different designs are painted as single motifs in the panels in the centre illustration. The variations in the shell forms add an element of subtlety.
MURALIST: GRAHAM RUST

▲ **A trompe l'œil frieze** in contrasting tones creates a lively three-dimensional effect of ornate relief plasterwork of entwined leaves. A frieze with a design such as this might be painted below a cornice or in a broad band all round a room in a period house.
MURALIST: ROBERT O'DEA

▼ **This image** of a broken terracotta pot from ancient Greece inspired a series of similar trompe l'œil fragments which the artist painted around the walls of a dining room.
MURALIST: ROBERT O'DEA

▼ **Inspired by ancient Greece, this vase** is part of a mural on a classical Greek theme for a hallway. The mural is composed of several sections, each having a different image. The motif in this detail was taken from an image of an Etruscan vase. The muralist distressed the finished painting to simulate aging.
MURALIST: RICHARD BAGGULEY

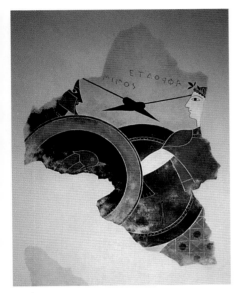

▲ **A painted plaster relief frames a lovely oval** trompe l'œil ceiling. The motif in the central corner panel was inspired by the work of a French designer of the 1700s, and was commissioned by the Marquess of Buckingham for the decorative scheme of the State Music Room at Stowe.
MURALIST: CAROLINE COWLEY

▲ **The decorative detail on this column** was inspired by a Roman example in a wall painting in the bedroom of a first century A.D. villa at Boscoreale near Pompeii, Italy. The original was coloured in the brilliant Pompeian red, with flowers in green and gold. The modern version is lighter and more restrained.
MURALIST: GARTH BENTON

138

▼ **Musical instruments are challenging subjects** for painters. Here, the artist observed the direction of a nearby light source in reproducing reflections in the instrument's curves and painting the shadows it casts.
MURALIST: PETER WHITEMAN

▼ **Charming details such as this** beautifully painted door handle prolong the enjoyment of a mural and play a role in convincing the viewer of the illusory effect of a larger trompe l'œil.
MURALIST: MARIE BYNG

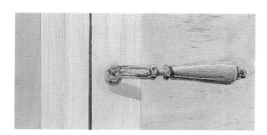

▼ **An urn of enamelled metal** sits alongside a miscellany of other objects on a cupboard in a trompe l'œil mural. It creates visual interest and its painted shadow enhances the three-dimensional effect.
MURALIST: PETER WHITEMAN

▲ **Little details** in murals, such as small animals and insects, often escape notice for some time. Only when the impact of the first impression has been absorbed does the viewer begin to discover these contributions to the visual story, often with complete surprise. They add to the fascination of a mural and play an important role in prolonging its fascination for the owner.
MURALIST: CATHERINE PERRYMAN

▲ **Collections** of thematically related and visually interesting objects may be painted on the doors of rooms and cupboards in attractive hanging arrangements. This assemblage of musical motifs is a self-contained decorative detail painted on a door panel.
MURALIST: GARTH BENTON

▲ **Humour and wit** are an absorbing component of many surface paintings. Small, isolated subjects, such as these shells depicted in realistic detail, may play amusing visual tricks on the flat surfaces around a house or in an apartment.
MURALIST: CRISTOPHE DE CARPENTERIE

▼ **A tame macaw carrying a message for a diner** is the focal point of a table which is the central feature of a dining room scene. Birds have always been popular subjects for murals, as points of interest and colour in large paintings and as decorative subjects for small, self-contained ones in isolated areas.
MURALIST: GARTH BENTON

▼ **Perched on an old wall,** its back to the viewer, this exquisitely painted bird lends a pensive air to an atmospheric mural. The artist has captured in fine detail the weightless quality of the creature's tiny body and the softness of its feathers.
MURALIST: RENZO MONGIARDINO

▲ **A watchful magpie** perched on an urn has been used by a muralist to create striking foreground detail. This makes a superb contrast with the fresh green lawn of an immaculate garden.
MURALIST: ZOE CRIPPS

▲ **Exotic birds with wings outstretched** make excellent material for studies of graceful avian poses. The attractive colouring and languid movement of a long-legged spoonbill provide pleasing and visually lively contrast against the cooler colours of the static sculpture.
MURALIST: GRAHAM RUST

the muralists

The author and publishers have made every effort to credit the muralists whose work is featured in this book. Unfortunately, however, we have been unable to trace those muralists whose names are not included below.

Richard Bagguley
58a Emmanuel Road
London SW12 0HP
Tel: (020) 8673 5949
Richard Bagguley undertakes commissions for all types of murals, and places special emphasis on classical themes. His work also incorporates specialist paint effects, and he gives advice on how best to present a mural in interior design.

Helen Barnes
3 The Crescent
Pendleton Road
Redhill
Surrey RH1 6LD
Tel: (01737) 241549
Murals and trompe l'œil.

Sophia Barratt
Painted Illusions
24 Ladbroke Gardens
London SW11 2PY
Tel/fax: (0171) 727 1595
Sophia Barratt trained in fine art and now specializes in imagined environments, often using architectural frameworks. She and her team welcome enquiries from private and corporate clients from the UK and abroad.

Garth Benton
PO Box 1064
Pebble Beach, CA 93953
USA
Tel: (408) 372 7457
&
PO Box 454
Headland, AL 36345
USA
Tel: (334) 693 3557
Diversity best describes Garth Benton's work, as he is called upon by architects and interior designers to paint pastiches of different historical periods and styles.

Jonathan Brunskill
140 Battersea Park Road
London SW11 4NB
Decorative artwork and murals in keeping with period interiors.

Marie Byng
35 rue de Seine
75006 Paris
France
Tel: (00331) 46 34 02 76
Marie Byng paints a range of decorative effects, including wood and marble, and reproduces natural landscapes. She specializes in a plaster effect called 'à la chaux'. This is plaster with pigments which is spread on a wall, sanded, and then waxed for a beautiful effect. She undertakes private and commercial commissions.

Ian Cairnie
32 Elms Avenue
London N10 2JP
Tel: (020) 8883 2569
Work includes all kinds of decorative and mural painting. Particularly known for highly detailed trompe l'œil work on a large and small scale. Enjoys commissions from clients who have particular requests for specific objects or locations to be included in the painting.

Rebecca Campbell
401 and ½ Workshops
401 and ½ Wandsworth Rd
London SW8 2JP
Tel: (020) 7622 5231
Website:
www.rebeccacampbell.co.uk
Muralist, illustrator, and designer.

David Carter
David Carter Interior Design
109 Mile End Road
London E1 4UJ
Tel: (020) 7790 0259
Website: www.alacarter.com
Trendsetting and innovative creator of some of the most memorable rooms in domestic interiors in recent years. Offers a complete interior design service.

Bruce Church
The Studio
11a Pembridge Crescent
London W11 3DT
Tel: (020) 7229 0564
Private and commercial commissions, working in London, New York, USA, and France. Largely architectural paintings which are scrupulously researched and from a wide range of periods.

Ricardo Cinalli
Beaux Arts
22 Cork Street
London W1X 3NA
Tel: (020) 7437 5799
Represented by the Beaux Arts gallery.

Caroline Cowley
at Titley and Marr
Unit 7, Chelsea Harbour
Design Centre
London SW10 0XE
Tel: (020) 7351 2913
Specialist decoration and design.

Zöe Cripps
Flat 1
35 Callcott Road
London NW6 7EE
Tel: (020) 7625 4915
Specializes in painting faux fireplaces and windows.

Davies, Keeling, Trowbridge Ltd (DKT)
3 Charterhouse Works
Eltringham Street
London SW18 1TD
Tel: (020) 8874 3565
Specialist decoration.

Alan Dodd
295 Caledonian Road
London N1 1ET
Tel: (020) 7607 8737
Alan Dodd's work extends the architectural setting with a timelessness rooted in the great traditions of decorative painting.

Christopher Drew
22 Burland Road
London SW11
Tel: (020) 7223 6265 (UK);
(00335) 5305 8280
(France)

Much of Christopher Drew's work is inspired by historical references. He designs and paints murals for interiors, and paints furniture, in the UK and in France.

Colin Failes
6 Elfindale Road
London SE24 9NW
Tel: (020) 7274 2093
Specializes in trompe l'œil and murals for interiors. Small-scale trompe l'œil works can be painted on canvas or wooden panels.

Peter Farlow
34 Kensington Church St
London W8 4HA
Tel: (020) 7937 3388
Email: peterfarlow@
compuserve.com
Period specialist decoration and trompe l'œil. A wide range of finishes, including graining and gilding.

Richard Gillette
407 Greenwich Street,
New York, NY 10013
Tel/fax: (212) 226 3850
Richard Gillette's approach to interior design is to use tactile surfaces and monochromatic colour schemes to unify diverse styles and periods, and eclectic themes.

Roberta Gordon-Smith
Artyfacts,
10 Lysia Street
London SW6 6NG
Tel: (020) 7381 0601
Trompe l'œil murals.

Veere Grenney
Veere Grenney Associates
1b Hollywood Road
London SW10 9HS
Tel: (020) 7351 7170
Interior designer.

Richard Haas
Richard Haas Inc
361 West 36th Street
New York, NY 10018
USA
Tel: (212) 947 9868
Richard Haas has been involved in designing and executing public and private architectural paintings for 25 years, and has completed more than 120 projects to date.

Anthony Kowalski
1 Wellesly Road
London W4 4BJ
Anthony Kowalski asks his clients to imagine their wall full of symbolic images, questions and answers, and reflections of themselves.

Josephine Lely
Calle Major 3
Berdun
Huesca
Spain 22770
Tel: (0034) 74 37 17 34
&
80 St Clement's Hill
Norwich
Norfolk NR3 4BW
Tel: (01603) 425546
Paints in oils. Specializes in tropical scenes depicting wildlife, marine life, and fantasy.

Catherine Lovegrove
Studio K4, Cooper House
2 Michael Road
Fulham
London SW6 2AD
Tel: (020) 7371 7814
Website: www.clmurals.com
Established for more than 12 years. She usually carries out her work in her own studios and installs it complete at the client's premises.

Mimi O'Connell
Port of Call Ltd
13 Walton Street
London W11
Tel: (020) 7589 4836
Fax: (020) 7823 9828
Mimi O'Connell likes to express in her decorations a feeling of fantasy and affordable splendour based, like all her work, on harmonious, disciplined elegance.

Robert O'Dea
50 Brawne House
Brandon Estate
London SE17
Tel: (020) 7582 1367
Robert O'Dea works with interior designers and architects on private and public commissions in the UK and internationally. He paints murals, panels, screens, canvasses and furniture, in a broad range of images and styles.

Catherine Perryman
85 Beaconsfield Villas
Brighton BN1 6HF
Specialist decoration, mural painting and tile panels.

Jayne Pope
103 Hampton Road
London E7 0NX
Tel: (020) 8534 3555
Commissions include work in private houses, specializing in the Renaissance and Pre-Raphaelite periods, and Indian images and styles.

Tony Raymond
8 Wolsey Road
London N8 8RP
Tel: (020) 8341 2829
Exotic and sumptuous 17th- and 18th-century murals and decorations.

Richmond International
Chapter House
22 Chapter Street
London SW1P 4NP
Tel: (020) 7828 6123
Interior designers.

Stephen Roberts
107 Howard House
Dolphin Square
London SW1V 3PE
Tel: (020) 7798 8137
Stephen Roberts uses mainly representational themes for his murals. He also specializes in trompe l'œil, portrait painting, and woodgraining, marbling, and other paint effects.

Graham Rust
Studio 7
49 Roland Gardens
London SW7 3PG
Graham Rust lives and works in South Kensington, London, and in Suffolk in eastern England. His published works include The Painted House *and* Decorative Designs - *see Bibliography, page 142.*

Lincoln Seligman
22 Ravenscourt Park
London W6 0TJ
Tel: (020) 8748 4670
Commissions have mostly included corporate and institutional buildings.

Janet Shearer
Higher Grogley Farm
Withiel
Nr Bodmin
Cornwall PL30 5NP
Tel: (01208) 831 926
Janet Shearer is renowned for her trompe l'œils and her murals. Her work is distinguished by minute architectural accuracy. She is passionate about animals, especially horses, which she paints superbly. She welcomes students to stay at her farm and study the art of trompe l'œil in her large, daylight studio.

Sebastian Wakefield
Cam Laithe, Far Lane
Kettlewell, Skipton
North Yorkshire BD23 5QY
Tel: (01756) 760809
Applied artist and restorer.

Peter Whiteman
3 Station Terrace
Twyford
Berks RG10 9NE
Designer and technician working for theatre, films, museums and exhibitions. Now specializing as a muralist extensively in Italy.

Additional Sources
Ritins Studio Inc
170 Wickstead Avenue
Toronto
Ontario
Canada M49 2B6
Tel: (416) 467 8920
Fax: (416) 467 8963
Engaged in decorative painting and faux finishing for 23 years. Also a School of Applied Decorative Arts and Design, many of its 4,000 graduates have gone on to generate their own businesses.

acknowledgements

The author and publishers would like to thank all muralists and artists for their kind assistance and permission to reproduce photographs of their work; the owners of the murals, with special thanks to: Mr and Mrs Robert Fisher, (pages 24-25); Mr and Mrs Eric and Ronna Hoffman (pages 34-35) and Mr and Mrs Henry Singleton and interior designer Laura Mako (pages 40-41). We would also like to give special thanks to Garth Benton for his kindness and generosity in providing photographs of his work at short notice.

bibliography

Cass, Caroline, *Grand Illusions: Contemporary Interior Murals* (Phaidon, UK, 1988; Chronicle Books, USA, 1993)

Chambers, Karen S., *Trompe l'Oeil* (Cassell, UK 1991; Rizzoli, USA, 1991)

Dars, Celestine, *Images of Deception* (Phaidon, UK, 1979)

Gordon-Smith, Roberta, *Trompe l'Oeil Techniques* (David & Charles, UK, 1997)

Milman, Miriam, *Trompe l'Oeil Painting* (Macmillan, UK, 1983; Skira/Rizzoli, USA, 1983)

Milman, Miriam, *Trompe l'Oeil: Painted Architecture* (Skira/Rizzoli, USA, 1986)

Plant, Tim, *Painted Illusions: A Creative Guide to Painting Murals and Trompe l'Oeil Effects* (Ward Lock, UK, 1991; Sterling, USA, 1991)

Rust, Graham, *The Painted House* (Macmillan, UK, 1988; Knopf, USA, 1988)

Rust, Graham, *Decorative Designs* (Cassell, UK, 1996)

Seligman, Patricia, *Painting Murals* (Little, Brown and Company, UK, 1993)

Fleming, John and Honour, Hugh, *A World History of Art* (Laurence King Publishing, UK, 1995)

photographic credits

Front Cover: Mint/Elizabeth Whiting Associates; 2 Eddie Royle-Hodges; 3 Robert O'Dea; 5 Garth Benton; 6 T Jeanson/Stock Image; 7 Garth Benton; 8-9 Donald V Bowling; 10 Schulenburg/The Interior Archive; 11 Bruce Church; 13 Richard Bagguley; 14 t DKT; 14 b Bulloz; 16 Tim Street-Porter/Elizabeth Whiting Associates;17 James Mortimer/The Interior Archive; 18-19 Visual Arts Library/Porteurs d'offrandes - scene de boucherie/Louvre ; 19 Scala - Florence; 19 inset Richard Bagguley; 20-21 Scala-Florence 22 E T Archive/National Palace, Mexico; 24-25 Garth Benton; 27 Elizabeth Whiting Associates; 28 Rebecca Campbell; 29 Robert O'Dea; 30-31 Schulenburg/The Interior Archive; 32 Rodney Hyett/Elizabeth Whiting Associates; 33 Schulenburg/The Interior Archive; 34-35 Todd Vitti; 34 b Angelo Hornak; 35 Todd Viitti; 36-37 Robert O'Dea; 38 Mick Hurd/Elizabeth Whiting Associates; 39 James Mortimer/The Interior Archive; 40-41 Todd Vitti; 42-43 Schulenburg/The Interior Archive; 44 Jean Vertut; 45 l Catherine Perryman; 45 r Suzanne Board; 46-47 Josephine Lely; 48-49 Robert O'Dea; 50-51 Rebecca Campbell; 52 Suzanne Board; 53 Schulenburg/The Interior Archive; 54 Robert O'Dea; 55 Richard Haas; 57 Ray Main/Mainstream Photography; 58 Lucinda Lambton/Arcaid; 60-61 Ian Cairnie;62 Jonathan Brunskill; 63 Alex Ramsay; 65 b Caroline Cowley; 65 t Werner Forman Archive/Museo Nazionale Romano, Rome; 66 Ian Cairnie; 68 Helen Barnes; 69 Marie Byng; 70 Richard Bagguley; 71 Colin Failes; 72 E T Archive; 73 Lincoln Seligman; 74 Elizabeth Whiting Associates; 75 Colin Failes; 76 Peter Mauss; 77 t Schulenburg/ The Interior Archive; 77 b DKT; 79 Peter Mauss; 81 t Peter Mauss; 81b Catherine Lovegrove; 82-83 Stephen Roberts; 84 Peter Mauss; 85 t Colin Failes; 85 b DKT; 86-87 Elizabeth Whiting Associates; 88-89 Eddie Ryle-Hodges; 90 Caroline Cowley; 91 Schulenburg/The Interior Archive; 92 Eddie Ryle-Hodges; 93 Peter Whiteman; 94 Elizabeth Whiting Associates; 96 G. de Laubier; 97 Lucinda Lambton/Arcaid; 98-99 Schulenburg/The Interior Archive; 100-101 Lorenzo Lees; 102 E T Archive/Palazzo Ducale, Mantua;103 DKT;104 Elizabeth Whiting Associates; 107 Photographie Bulloz; 108 Peter Mauss; 109 t Schulenburg/The Interior Archive; 109 b Christopher Drew; 110-111 Richard Bryant/Arcaid; 112-113 Schulenburg/ The Interior Archive; 115 t Robert O'Dea; 115 b James Mortimer/ The Interior Archive; 116 Caroline Cowley; 117 Robert O'Dea; 118 l Peter Mauss; 118 r Colin Failes; 119 Sophia Barratt; 120 Ray Main/ Mainstream Photography; 122-123 Ian Cairnie; 124 Schulenburg/The Interior Archive; 125 Jonathan Brunskill; 127-129 Stephen Roberts; 130 Garth Benton; 131 Sebastian Wakefield; 133 Garth Benton;134 l Ray Main/Mainstream Photography; 134 centre top Tim Street-Porter/Elizabeth Whiting Associates; 134 tr Anthony Kowalski; 134 b Marie Byng; 135 tl and tr Ian Cairnie and Tony Raymond; 135 top centre Caroline Cowley; 135 centre below Garth Benton; 136 l Ian Cairnie; 136 tr Inside, Boulogne, France; 136 centre Ken Kirkwood; 136 b Robert O'Dea; 137 tl Robert O'Dea; 137 centre top Richard Bagguley; 137 r Garth Benton; 137b Caroline Cowley; 138 tl and tr Peter Whiteman; centre top Marie Byng; 138 bl Catherine Perryman; 138 centre below Garth Benton; 138 br J Darblay/Inside, Boulogne, France; 139 tl Garth Benton; 139 tr Schulenburg/The Interior Archive; 139 bl Zöe Cripps; 139 br Ken Kirkwood; Back cover: Elizabeth Whiting Associates

index

Page numbers in italics *(121)* refer to illustrations; a page number in bold type (**121**) refers to a major entry and a number in roman type (121) indicates a brief mention.